The German Food Book

PREPARING, COOKING & SERVING FOOD FROM GERMANY

JUDY RIDGWAY

A MARTIN  BOOK

Published by Martin Books
17 Market Street, Cambridge CB2 3PA
for the Central Marketing Organisation
of German Agricultural Industries
44–46 Knightsbridge, London SW1X 7JN

First published 1983

ISBN 0 85941 248 2

Design and layout: Ken Vail Graphic Design
Photography: Studio Teubner, Füssen, West Germany
Typesetting: Westholme Graphics Limited, Gamlingay, Beds
Origination: Anglia Reproductions, Witham, Essex
Printed and bound in Great Britain by
Balding + Mansell, Wisbech, Cambs

CONTENTS

INTRODUCTION

German food and drink have been staging a quiet takeover on our supermarket shelves in recent years. Have a look at almost any section and there is sure to be something from Germany. The selection of German foods is vast: sausages, hams and cold meats; breads and cheeses; canned fish, fruit and vegetables; mustards and pickles; noodles; dumpling and pancake mixes; and biscuits and confectionery, as well as fruit juices, beers and wines. The list seems endless, but even so it is only the tip of the iceberg of produce on sale in Germany itself.

German housewives take their food shopping very seriously and the one thing that they rate higher than anything else is quality. Indeed, everyone has a high regard for good food, and perhaps because of this Germany has many more specialist food shops than we have in Britain. These shops take a pride in the quality of their merchandise and vie with each other in the beauty and attractiveness of their displays.

On a recent vist to Munich, for instance, I was amazed and delighted to find seven or eight small butchers' shops side by side around the market place, each with a window that was more tantalising than the one before. The market, too, was a joy with permanent stalls selling mountains of crusty fresh bread and varieties of cheese, fruit and locally grown vegetables. Despite the genuine market atmosphere, quality was still the order of the day.

Fresh food markets and specialist food shops are to be found all over Germany, and even in the supermarkets fresh foods are sold from individual counters. Assistants in both the supermarkets and the smaller shops are trained so that they are knowledgeable about the food they are selling. There doesn't seem to be anything they don't know about the different varieties, origins and traditions of the products.

Germany, of course, has culinary traditions and regional specialities, some of which date back to the Middle Ages. But like those of most other European countries, German eating patterns keep pace with the times, and the modern trend towards a lighter cuisine is reflected in the top German restaurants. Again, the emphasis is on the quality of ingredients, which presents no problem in a country which introduced the very first food law as far back as 1516.

Today legislation ensures that all German sausages, for example, contain 100 per cent meat – more than can be said for the British banger, popular though it is!

With this sort of background it's not surprising that German food and drink sells so well in the United Kingdom. It is food which is appetising and appreciated by both the cook of the family and the family itself. But the full potential of German produce hasn't yet been fully realised in this country.

Most people in Britain, for example, know that sliced German sausages go well with bread and butter or with salads. But how many, I wonder, realise that they can also be used in soups, stews and casseroles, as kebabs or in fondues and in egg, cheese and vegetable dishes? They also work well in risottos, pasta dishes, omelettes and quiches. And this sort of wide-ranging application holds good for many other German foods as well.

Experimentation is the best way to get the most from German produce. Two air-dried salamis, two fresh sausages, two cheeses or two fruit juices may look the same but may taste very different. So try out as many as possible and get to know which ones you like best. The same applies to cooked dishes. Almost all sausage types, for example, are readily interchangeable though strengths of flavour and texture may influence the choice for a particular dish.

In this book I have tried to show how well German produce can fit into everyday British cooking. Some of my ideas have come from adaptations of German recipes, but most of them were inspired by the foods themselves and by modern family cooking in Britain.

In the chapter entitled 'Choosing German Specialities' I have tried to cover the German produce most commonly available in Britain so that if you buy a food which is unfamiliar to you, you can check on its characteristics, uses and storage. A look in the index should also point the way to some specific recipes using that item. Alternatively, you may come across an ingredient that you have not used before in one of the recipes, and then you can look it up in this reference chapter.

I have certainly had a lot of fun devising the recipes given here and learning about German food and I could not resist some of the traditional festive delicacies served at Christmas and New Year. Some of these you will find in the chapters on 'Entertaining German-style' and 'Traditional Festive Food'.

I hope you enjoy the food as much as I have!

NOTE:
- *All recipes serve four unless otherwise stated.*
- *All spoon measurements are level.*
- *All eggs are size 3 unless otherwise stated.*
- *Quantities of ingredients are given in both metric (g, ml) and imperial (oz, pint) measures; you can use either,* but not a mixture of both, *in any recipe.*

CHOOSING GERMAN SPECIALITIES

Whether you are looking for a change in the kind of sausages you buy, a new cheese to add to a party cheeseboard, a natural wholemeal loaf or a different fruit juice to start the day you need look no further than the fascinating range of German produce on sale in most supermarkets. If you have a specialist delicatessen nearby the choice will be even wider, taking in fish products, pickles, potato mixes, sweet biscuits, flans and cakes. Indeed, the selection is now so wide that you could be forgiven for not knowing quite what to choose.

Sometimes the problem also extends to the question of how to serve the food. Everyone knows that ham sausage can be sliced and served in a sandwich or with a salad, but it is also very good cut into chunks and used on kebabs or in hotpots and casseroles. And this kind of versatility applies to most German products on sale in Britain.

This chapter provides a round-up of some of the German foods most commonly available in this country, together with some notes on how to recognise, store and use them.

SAUSAGES

The number of sausages eaten in Germany each year is quite phenomenal, but there are good reasons for this high consumption.

First of all, German schools start quite early in the morning, and there are no school meals. Children take a packed sandwich meal with them for mid-morning breakfast; usually some sausage is included and sometimes some cheese. Children then go home for lunch, which in Germany is the main meal of the day. A hot dish is always prepared and this will often include sausages. Finally, the family sits down in the evening to a cold supper, which also makes great use of sliced meats and sausages. But despite the number of occasions in any one week when sausage may be eaten, German families never tire of them because there are so many varieties available.

Wurst is the general German name for sausage. There are now more than 80 different sausages or wurst on sale in Britain, although you won't find them all in the same shop or supermarket! So far I have come across about 50 of them. Try as many as you can, and remember that there is virtually no waste on any of them.

PRESERVED SLICING SAUSAGES

These sausages are made from fresh lean pork, bacon and beef, and are smoked and air-dried to give them a long life. They are sometimes known as 'dry' sausage and can usually be seen hanging behind the counter in shops and stores. However, they may also be sliced and sold in vacuum packs.

Some preserved sausages are made in the shape of a long loaf rather than a round sausage. Different spices and seasonings are used according to the specific recipes, many of which are regional in origin. Some contain garlic and others do not.

Storage: Hang uncut in a cool, airy, draught-free place. The temperature should be 15–18°C/60–65°F. If your kitchen is a warm one, store the uncut sausages in the bottom of the fridge. Cut slices should always be stored in the fridge.

Uses: Slice thinly, remove the skin and serve on bread or with salad. Alternatively, skin and dice and use to flavour soups, pasta and rice dishes and mixed salads.

Cervelat

This is a fine-textured sausage made from finely minced pork and beef. It is smoked to a golden-brown colour on the outside and is pinkish inside. The flavour is mild and delicate.

Very good in sandwiches and hors d'oeuvres, as toasted snacks with cheese and pizza toppings, and for flavouring vegetable dishes and salads. (See Index for specific recipes.)

Salami

Salami is also made from minced pork and beef but it has a coarser texture than cervelat. It is usually highly spiced and may contain garlic. The outer casing is often reddish-brown in colour and may be wrapped with a string mesh. Some salamis are darker and coated with peppercorns. The inside is darker in colour than cervelat and usually has a smoky flavour.

Very good in sandwiches and salads and as part of a cold meat platter. Its smoky flavour is also very good in thick soups, with potatoes and in quiches. (See Index for specific recipes.)

Katenrauchwurst *(Smoked cottage sausage)*

This is a coarse-textured, very firm sausage which undergoes a very long smoking process. It is made almost exclusively from pork and is fairly strongly flavoured. It goes well with dark rye bread such as pumpernickel.

Mettwurst

Made from mildly smoked pork and beef, these sausages may be fine or coarse in texture and some of them are soft enough to be spreadable. Their size also varies considerably. All those except the spreadable ones may be used in just the same way as salami or cervelat.

> *Key:*
> ① *Cervelat*
> ② *Salami*
> ③ *Pepper salami*
> ④ *Katenrauchwurst*
> ⑤ *Mettwurst*

FRESH SLICING SAUSAGES

These sausages, too, are made from finely minced pork, bacon and beef, but instead of being smoked and air-dried over a long period of time, they are very quickly smoked and then scalded at a high temperature to seal in the flavour. Like preserved sausages, the different flavours are achieved by the use of different spices and herbs and garlic. Fresh slicing sausages are usually very smooth, sometimes with larger chunks of meat in the fine mixture. They may be sold in slices or pieces from whole sausages or they may be vacuum-packed.

Storage: Keep in the fridge and eat within a day or two of purchase. Vacuum-packs, too, should be kept in the fridge. Use by the 'sell-by' date.

Uses: Slice and skin and use in sandwiches, cold meat platters and mixed salads. Thick slices can be fried or grilled. Cut into chunks and use in soups, casseroles and hotpots or thread on to kebab skewers and cook under the grill or over a barbecue.

Extrawurst *(Fleischwurst)*
This is a juicy, fine-textured and well-flavoured sausage. The sausage varies in diameter and may be pink to light brown in colour.

Very good cut into strips and used in mixed salads, as fillings for rolls and on open sandwiches. Heat in hot, not boiling, water and serve sliced with gravy and vegetables or fry in butter and serve with fried onions and grilled tomatoes. (See Index for specific recipes.)

Bierwurst *(Beer sausage)*
Despite its name, this sausage is made from a finely chopped mixture of pork and beef with no beer in the recipe at all. Its name actually drives from the fact that this particular sausage goes so well with beer. They have a fine texture, are pinkish-red in colour and are traditionally oval in shape. Some varieties contain garlic.

Very good in sliced cold meat platters, closed sandwiches and open sandwiches with pickles.

Serve hot as for extrawurst or cut into cubes and use in chowders, kebabs or hotpots. (See Index for specific recipes.)

Schinkenwurst *(Ham sausage)*
This well-textured sausage is made from beef and pork with chunks of ham and bacon. It has a spicy flavour and may contain garlic. Very good in sliced cold meat platters, salads and sandwiches. It can also be sliced and fried or grilled or cut into chunks and used in casseroles, soups and vegetable dishes. (See Index for specific recipes.)

This type of sausage must, by law, contain more than 50 per cent ham to be called schinkenwurst.

Bierschinken
This sausage is very similar to bierwurst but coarser with chunks of cooked ham in the mixture. Use cold in the same way as extrawurst and bierwurst but exercise care when using this sausage in hot dishes as the heat tends to bring

out the garlic flavour. Use in robust dishes with plenty of onions, tomatoes, potatoes or pasta. (See Index for specific recipes.)

Jagdwurst *(Hunter's sausage)*
This is another well-flavoured garlic sausage which is made from finely minced pork interlaced with small pieces of fat. Very good in salads and sandwiches and in hot spicy dishes like Sausage Goulash. (See Index for specific recipes.)

> **Key:**
> ⑥ *Extrawurst*
> ⑦ *Bierwurst*
> ⑧ *Schinkenwurst*
> ⑨ *Bierschinken*

COOKED SLICING SAUSAGES

These sausages are made from pre-cooked meats and liver or tongue and are flavoured with herbs, onions and spices. They may contain quite large pieces of meat making the cut surface very attractive in appearance.

Storage: Store in the fridge and eat as soon as possible.

Uses: Slice and skin and use in sandwiches or with salads. These sausages also help to make a cold sausage platter look even more varied and attractive.

Sülzwurst *(Brawn sausage)*
This contains large pieces of pork from the head or the leg, all held together in a savoury wine vinegar jelly. It is best if cut fairly thinly. Serve with salad or bread or on a mixed sausage platter.

Zungenwurst *(Tongue sausage)*
This is a tongue sausage containing whole pieces of tongue in a smoother mixture than sülzwurst. It is medium-spiced with black pepper. Best served with salad or bread or on a mixed sausage platter.

SPREADING SAUSAGES

These are soft sausages which are enclosed in skins of various kinds. The mixture is soft enough to spread easily on bread or biscuits. They may be smoked or cooked. See individual sausages for storage and use.

Teewurst
This is a preserved sausage made from a very finely minced mixture of pork and beef. It is spicy but delicate in flavour. It is usually packed into short sausages with reddish-brown skins. The meat is salmon pink in colour. Store in the fridge for up to a week.

Very good in sandwiches, on hot-buttered toast and on canapés. It can be used in stuffings for poultry or vegetables. (See Index for specific recipes.)

Leberwurst *(Liver sausage)*
German varieties are made from cooked liver and other meats. They may be packed as short or long sausages in a variety of casings. They usually contain onion and appropriate seasonings and are lightly smoked. The commonest variety is very smooth and fine. Others contain pork and bacon or veal as well as liver and are coarser in texture. Eat as soon after purchase as possible.

Very good on bread and in canapés and in any recipe which calls for liver pâté. It also makes an excellent stuffing for eggs, raw vegetables or pinwheel sandwiches. (See Index for specific recipes.)

Key:
① *Sülzwurst*
② *Zungenwurst*
③ *Teewurst*
④ *Leberwurst*

8

SMALL WHOLE SAUSAGES

Frankfurters are known world wide and they are typical of the range of small German sausages. They are made from fresh ingredients, lightly smoked and then scalded. Small sausages may be made from pork alone or from a mixture of pork and beef. They are available loose, vacuum-packed, canned or bottled.

In Germany they are sold ready-to-eat from small stalls in the streets and market places, and they certainly make a deliciously warming snack. In fact the Germans quite happily stand at these stalls in the freezing cold of winter enjoying a hot sausage and mustard with fresh bread.

Storage: If loose or vacuum-packed, keep in the fridge and eat within a day or two of purchase.

Uses: Some of the sausages can be grilled, others should be warmed through in hot, not boiling, water. The easiest method is to boil the water, remove from the heat and add the sausages for about five minutes. This prevents them from splitting. These sausages can also be sliced and used in cold salads or in hot soups, chowders and casseroles. In the latter recipes, always add the sausages at the end of the cooking time.

Frankfurters

Strictly speaking, sausages should be given the name frankfurter only if they are made in or around Frankfurt, but they are now made all over Germany. Frankfurters are made from top-quality lean pork with a small amount of salt, bacon fat and spices all ground together into a fine paste. This is then put into casings and the sausages are smoked, which gives a yellowish tinge to the skins. Do make sure that the frankfurters you buy really are German-made, as those manufactured in other countries simply do not have the same texture and flavour.

Very good as hot snacks or for supper with potatoes, potato salad or other vegetables. Warm through in hot water as described above. Slice and use in soups, salads and hotpots. (See Index for specific recipes.)

Knackwurst

These are very similar to frankfurters but they are likely to be shorter and plumper. The name stems from the fact that when they are heated and bent the skin splits with a cracking sound.

Bockwurst

These look very similar to frankfurters but are made from a mixture of finely ground beef and pork. They are smoked until they attain their traditional pink colour, and are usually larger in diameter than frankfurters. Use as for frankfurters. (See Index for specific recipes.)

Bratwurst

These are much paler in colour than frankfurters. They are frying or grilling sausages and are made from pure pork or veal, either finely or coarsely minced. Serve with bacon and tomato, scrambled eggs or baked beans for a nourishing supper or as part of a breakfast or brunch grill. They are also very good with potatoes and other vegetables as part of the main meal of the day.

> Key:
> ⑤ *Frankfurters*
> ⑥ *Knackwurst*
> ⑦ *Bockwurst*
> ⑧ *Bratwurst*

SPECIALITY MEATS

In addition to sausages, Germany produces a delicious range of smoked and cured meats. These include cured and air-dried hams, cooked hams, smoked beef and cured and smoked pork joints of various kinds.

Storage: Air-dried products in one piece, like air-dried sausages, can be stored in a cool and airy place for some time. Temperatures should be 15–18°C/60–65°F. However, you are probably more likely to buy these products already sliced. If they are loose, store in the fridge and eat as soon as possible. If they are vacuum-packed, use by the 'sell-by' date.

Cooked meats, too, should be kept in the fridge and used as quickly as possible.

Uses: Most of these products may be sliced and served on open sandwiches or in salads. Use them, too, for canapés and hors d'oeuvres. Some of the uncooked products such as speck are used in general cooking as a source of fat.

SMOKED AND AIR-DRIED HAMS

Smoked hams have been a German speciality since Roman times. They are cured, smoked and air-dried by age-old methods and each region has its own special recipes which give a unique flavour to the local hams. Sometimes it is the ingredients or the length of the cure which give the flavour. In other cases it is the type of wood used in the smoking process which makes the difference.

These hams should be sliced very thinly indeed and served in the same way as Parma or Bayonne ham. Try them with melon, pears or figs as a dinner starter or use them with a selection of cold meats and sliced sausages in a cold meat platter.

In Germany there are a dozen or more smoked and air-dried hams to choose from. So far only two or three have found their way into our shops, but there are more on the way. Here are the two most frequently found.

Westphalian ham

This is probably the best known of these hams. It is made from a boneless piece of pork which is cured naturally with salt and brine and left to mature for three weeks or so in a cool cellar. It is then smoked over resin-free woods to which juniper berries have been added. This process, too, takes weeks to give the characteristic dark colour and smoky flavour. The ham may be left as an irregularly shaped piece or it may be rolled to give symmetrical rounds. Either way, the ham should be sliced very thinly for serving.

Very good eaten just as it is with brown bread and butter or served with melon or other fruit. Small pieces can be used in mixed salads, hors d'oeuvres and canapés or can be wrapped around pieces of vegetables and mayonnaise. (See Index for specific recipes.)

Black Forest ham

This is a traditional air-dried ham from Southern Germany. It has a much stronger and smokier flavour than Westphalian ham. Try it on open sandwiches with potato salad or with coleslaw.

Boiled Black Forest ham is also available in Britain.

> **Key:**
> ① *Westphalian ham*
> ② *Black Forest ham*
> ③ *Boiled Black Forest ham*

COOKED HAMS

A variety of cooked hams are imported by Britain from Germany. Their flavour varies according to the type of cure used and the length of time the ham is cooked. The quality of German hams is usually very high as they do not contain any added water.

CURED PORK

Kassler

This is loin of pork lightly salted, pickled in brine and then smoked. The addition of juniper berries during the smoking process adds to the flavour of the meat, though it is still fairly mild.

Use thinly sliced and roll round asparagus or other fillings, or add to a meat platter or to hors d'oeuvres or canapés. Large pieces can be oven-roasted, glazed and served with fruit.

Lachsschinken

This is a mildly cured and smoked loin of pork which is cut into small pieces and rolled in sheets of bacon fat to preserve the moisture and flavour.

Use very thinly sliced and serve as an hors d'oeuvre with horse-radish sauce or use in canapés, open sandwiches and food for special occasions.

Speck

Speck is the German word for bacon but it usually refers to mildly cured and smoked pork fat. It may be used in the same way as bacon fat.

Katenspeck

This is similar to speck but includes some lean meat. It resembles streaky bacon but the flavour is quite different and, unlike English bacon, it is cooked. Slices may be eaten cold or it may be used in cooked dishes in just the same way as streaky bacon. (See Index for specific recipes.)

Key:
④ *Cooked ham*
⑤ *Kassler*
⑥ *Lachsschinken*
⑦ *Speck*
⑧ *Katenspeck*

CHEESE

Germany is one of the largest producers of dairy products in the world and although a good deal of this production is concentrated on butter, cheese is not far behind. German families eat quite a lot of cheese and their total consumption is double that of the UK.

There is a very wide range of cheeses to choose from in Germany, but half of all German cheese sales are in just one variety – quark soft cheese.

Quark has only recently appeared in British shops and we have not yet discovered all the many ways of using it. In Germany the cook of the family knows that it can be used in anything from a light and creamy dessert or a Continental cheesecake to a salad dressing or a topping for jacket potatoes. It's also delicious mixed with herbs, chopped vegetables or fruit and spread on bread.

The range of German cheeses in our shops is growing all the time. They all look good on a mixed cheeseboard but they can also be used in all kinds of cooking. Some of the hard cheeses go beautifully stringy when cooked and the semi-hard or sliceable cheeses add flavour and texture. Even the soft cheeses like German flavoured and blue bries can be used to make creamy soups and sauces.

HARD CHEESES

These, as their name implies, are hard, firm cheeses with a low water content which means that they have good keeping qualities.

Storage: They can be stored for much longer than other types of cheese. Wrap in foil or cling film and keep in the fridge. These cheeses do not freeze well in large pieces but they can be grated and frozen for up to three months.

Uses: On cheeseboards and sliced in open and closed sandwiches and toasted snacks. Cut into chunks or sticks to use in salads and canapés, and grate to use in all kinds of cooked dishes.

Allgäu emmentaler

This is sometimes known as schweizer käse or Swiss cheese because it originated in Switzerland. German emmentaler comes from the Allgäu or Alp regions in the south. It is very large, round cheese which may weight up to 90 kg and has a dark yellow rind. Inside the cheese is smooth matt yellow with well-distributed cherry-sized holes. Its flavour is mild and nutty, though it becomes a little stronger with age.

Use for rarebit mixtures, cheese sauces, fondue, omelettes and all kinds of savoury dishes (see Index for specific recipes). Buy in chunks and slice, chop or grate at home or buy ready-sliced cheese for sandwiches and hot toasted snacks.

Bergkäse

This is very similar to Allgäu emmentaler but with smaller holes and a more solid appearance. It also has a rather more robust flavour.

SLICEABLE CHEESES

These are a little softer than the hard cheeses but though pliable they are still firm enough to slice with a knife. Their flavour is very mild and they keep well.

Storage: Wrap in foil or cling film and keep in the fridge. Freeze sliced and store for up to three months.

Uses: On cheeseboards and in open and closed sandwiches and hot toasted snacks. Grate and use in cooked dishes of all kinds to give a very smooth effect.

Tilsiter

Originally from East Prussia, this is a pale yellow cheese which is available with and without a rind. Its texture is punctuated with small, uneven holes and it is mildly pungent and creamy tasting. Sometimes it can be found flavoured with caraway seeds.

Use sliced for open sandwiches, canapés and toasted snacks. Chop or grate for use in sauces and savoury dishes. Buy in pieces or vacuum-packed in slices. (See Index for specific recipes.)

Edam and gouda

These essentially Dutch cheeses are now produced all over Germany. The German cheeses are similar to their Dutch cousins except that the edam may be loaf-shaped. They are ideal for slicing and give a slightly stringy effect to cooked dishes.

Pilzkäse

This is a blue cheese which is strongly flavoured and rindless. The texture is crumbly and the colour is very white with blue-green veins which give a marbled effect.

Use on a cheeseboard or in canapés and sauces. (See Index for specific recipes.)

Key:
① Edam
② Tilsiter
③ Allgäu emmentaler
④ Bergkäse
⑤ Gouda
⑥ Pilzkäse

SMOKED CHEESES

These are firm processed cheeses which have been wood-smoked. They are very good on their own with biscuits or bread, or can be used to give a smoky cheese flavour to cooked dishes like macaroni cheese or Welsh rarebit. One variety of smoked cheese comes with little pieces of chopped ham mixed in.

READY-SLICED CHEESES

These are processed cheeses which are made from hard or sliceable cheeses. They are melted, mixed with a variety of flavourings, such as green and red peppers, and then sliced and packed in batches of four or six. Try them with snacks and toasted sandwiches and for topping grills and hamburgers.

Storage: Wrap in foil or cling film or leave in its own wrappings and store in the fridge. Eat by the 'sell-by' date.

SOFT CHEESES

These are soft spreadable cheeses. Each has its own distinctive shape, appearance and flavour. They are best when fresh and should not be kept for too long. When over-ripe they tend to become very soft and runny.

Storage: Wrap well in foil or cling film and store in the fridge. Freeze whole and store for up to three months.

Uses: On a cheeseboard and in open and closed sandwiches. Chop and use in cooked dishes for a very creamy effect.

Limburger

This is quite difficult to find in the UK but is worth the search. It has a distinctive aromatic flavour and smell which is quite pungent. It is pale creamy yellow in colour and the texture is smooth and slightly shiny. Its reddish-brown skin and small loaf shape make it a most attractive addition to the cheeseboard.

Camembert and brie

These two cheeses have been produced in Germany for many years. They are slightly milder than their French counterparts, and many of the bries are flavoured with herbs, mixed peppers or green peppercorns. Creamy blue bries have also been introduced with great success. In fact, they have joined the lists of top-selling cheeses in some of our supermarkets. Brie and camembert can be used in a great many dishes. Very often these cheeses are cut into wedges and are then individually wrapped and labelled.

Very good on cheeseboards and in open and closed sandwiches. Remove the rind and use to make very creamy soups, sauces and canapés. (See Index for specific recipes.)

CHEESE SPREADS

These cheeses are made from a variety of cheeses such as Allgäu emmentaler, gouda or edam which are melted down when sufficiently ripe and combined with butter and specified quantities of other ingredients such as chopped sausage, tomato concentrate, paprika, nuts, peppers, herbs and spices.

QUARK AND CREAM CHEESES

These are a group of cheeses made from skimmed milk, whole milk and whole milk plus cream. The range most commonly available is called quark. This comes in three levels of fat content, the lowest of which, at around 100 calories per 100 g (4 oz), can be very useful if you are on a slimming diet.

Quark is smooth and thick with a texture somewhere between that of yogurt and cream cheese. In cooking quark behaves as a cheese and can be used with excellent results to make cheesecakes, curd tarts and puddings. It can often be used in place of cream or mixed with cream to go with fruit, to line fruit flans or to fill cakes and pastries. Its savoury uses include cold dressings and sauces, dips and canapé fillings as well as stuffings and toppings for vegetable dishes (see Index for specific recipes).

Key:
⑦ *Ready-sliced cheese*
⑧ *Limburger*
⑨ *Smoked cheese*
⑩ *Quark*
⑪ *Flavoured bries*
⑫ *Camembert*
⑬ *Assorted cheese spreads*

BREAD

Whole-grain bread is very much the order of the day in Germany and white bread as we know it is unusual. Most German bread is made from rye flour, unlike our own which uses predominantly wheat flour. The lovely bakers' shops in Germany sell a really huge range of fresh bread and they are all quite delicious. Flavourings are used quite a lot, too, and these might be anything from poppy seeds and caraway seeds to herbs and spices.

Bread is not very easy to export as it goes stale quickly. Nevertheless, some German breads are specially double-wrapped and shipped on a regular basis to the UK.

Landbrot (*Farm bread*)
This is a brown bread made from rye and wholemeal flour which is leavened with typically German sour dough. The loaves are usually oval in shape and may be sold whole or sliced. Sometimes the slices are so large that they need to be halved or quartered for use.

Vollkornbrot
This is a full-grain rye bread which is darkish in colour though not as dark and strong as pumpernickel. It has a smooth, glazed surface and comes packed in slices. Use as for pumpernickel.

Leinsamenbrot
This is a healthy bread made from wholemeal flour and linseeds. It has a very coarse texture but the flavour is mild and delicious. It goes particularly well with liver sausage or pâté.

Pumpernickel (*Black bread*)
This is the general term given to coarse rye wholemeal bread. It is cooked in steam chambers for 20 hours enclosed in long rectangular tins to give it its traditional shape. It is this long cooking process which gives it the dark colour and strong, rich flavour. It is always sliced thinly and sold in packs of 225 g (8 oz), usually about eight slices. Serve with plenty of butter and cheese or sausage, or use for open sandwiches or canapés. (See Index for specific recipes.)

Knäckebrot (*Crispbread*)
This may be made from both rye and wheat flours. The dough contains very little water and is kneaded to trap pockets of air in it before undergoing a special baking process. This produces a very crisp texture.

Pretzels
These are dry salted biscuits, sometimes flavoured with caraway seeds. They may be shaped with the traditional knot or they may be long thin sticks. They are excellent served with cocktails, wine and beer.

Key:
① Landbrot
② Vollkornbrot
③ Leinsamenbrot
④ Pumpernickel
⑤ Knäckebrot
⑥ Salt sticks
⑦ Pretzels

BISCUITS AND CAKES

No round-up of German baking would be complete without mention of the biscuits and cakes, and an extensive range of both can be bought in Britain.

German biscuits are lighter and prettier than most English biscuits and include a mouthwatering variety of ingredients, such as almonds and hazelnuts, praline fillings, honey and real fruit essences and preserves. And if they come covered in chocolate, you can be sure it's the real thing and good and thick.

In Germany biscuits are served with morning or afternoon coffee, and they also make good petits fours.

Many shops and supermarkets in Britain now stock a variety of German biscuits, and several sizes of feather-light sponge layers and flan cases which take all the hard work out of preparing family puddings or special desserts for entertaining.

At Christmas even more variety appears with the addition of traditional stollen (also called Christstollen), and lebkuchen. Stollen is traditional German Christmas cake. It is made from a rich yeast dough, almonds, marzipan, butter, orange and lemon juice, candied peel and raisins, and is oval-shaped. The whole cake is dredged with icing sugar. Lebkuchen is gingerbread and comes in all sorts of shapes and sizes, some decorated with chocolate, icing sugar, crystallised fruits and nuts.

FRUIT JUICES

A very wide range of fruit juices is made and drunk in Germany and many of them now find their way to Britain. Apple juice is one of the most popular and may be drunk on its own at breakfast or indeed at any time of the day. Use it also in fruit cups and hot punches or as a partner to gin, white rum or vodka. Grape juices, too, both red and white, are commonly available. The range also includes apricot and peach juices, which have a little of the fruit purée added to give a full rich texture, and clear plum, cherry and blackcurrant juices.

Apple juice and red and white grape juices are really pure juices and do not contain any additives at all. Some of the others contain a little added water to improve their consistency, and one or two of the sharper fruits, like blackcurrant, have added sugar.

COMPLETING THE PICTURE

Fish products

Fish is traditionally associated with the area between the North and Baltic Seas and herrings are by far the most popular variety, although fish like cod, eel, haddock and salmon are also available, usually smoked.

Most of the herring products are canned, salted or pickled. Look out for rollmops which are pickled and rolled up with onions rather like a Swiss roll. They come in jars of various sizes. Rather similar are Bismarck herrings, but these are left in straight fillets and packed with the onions into taller jars. Matjes herrings look and taste different and are kept in brine or in a wine pickle. They are softer than Bismarck or rollmop herrings. All are very good in salads, hors d'oeuvres or open sandwiches.

Sauerkraut

Sauerkraut is possibly one of the most famous German foods. In the past German housewives prided themselves on making their own sauerkraut at home, often to traditional family recipes, but today most people buy their sauerkraut in jars or cans. It is served regularly in Germany and the average person eats about 2 kg (4 lb) a year.

Sauerkraut was originally devised as a way of keeping vitamin- and mineral-packed white cabbage through the winter. The cabbage is mixed with salt and wine and left to ferment. It is high in vitamin C, iron, calcium and phosphorus; careful processing by the manufacturers ensures that this goodness is kept intact to draw on at any time. Sauerkraut will keep for many years in unopened jars or cans.

In Germany sauerkraut is a must with small, hot sausages and with kassler. Try it, too, with gammon steaks, roast bacon joints or any kind of grilled or roast pork.

Other vegetables

There are many other bottled and canned vegetables. Look out for baby sweetcorn heads, asparagus, celeriac sticks and pfifferlinge. The latter is a mushroom-like fungus.

Mustards and pickles

Mustards and pickles, too, are widely available. German mustards are generally not hot and are often sweeter than English mustards. German pickles tend to have a sweet–sour flavour as sugar is included in the pickling liquor. Large gherkins and pickled cucumbers are particularly popular.

FAMILY FARE

CHICKEN SOUP WITH CHEESE DUMPLINGS

1 small boiling fowl (approx. 1 kg (2 lb)) with giblets
1 onion, chopped
1 carrot, diced
1 leek, turnip or swede as available, diced
1 bay leaf
sprigs of parsley and thyme
salt and pepper
1½ litres (2½ pints) water
15 ml spoon (1 tablespoon) chopped fresh parsley, to serve
Dumplings
100 g (4 oz) full-fat German quark
1 egg, beaten
15 ml spoon (1 tablespoon) butter, melted
200 g (7 oz) plain flour
salt
2 × 15 ml spoon (2 tablespoons) chopped fresh parsley

Place all the soup ingredients except the chopped parsley in a large pan and bring to the boil. Cover and simmer for at least 2 hours. If the chicken is cooked after this time, remove it and serve sliced with vegetables or leave it to cool and serve with salad.

Continue boiling the broth until it has reduced to 900 ml (1½ pints). If you like a chunky soup, leave the vegetables in it; otherwise strain the soup through muslin and return the liquid to the pan.

To make the dumplings, mix the quark, egg and melted butter to a smooth paste. Mix in the flour, salt and parsley and knead to a smooth dough. Break off small pieces and, with floured hands, roll into balls. Poach these in the chicken soup for 8–10 minutes until cooked through. Serve sprinkled with chopped parsley.

GREEN PEA SOUP WITH SEMOLINA DUMPLINGS

50 g (2 oz) German butter
450 g (1 lb) shelled (or frozen) peas
15 ml spoon (1 tablespoon) plain flour
350 g (12 oz) potatoes, diced
pinch of mixed herbs
salt and pepper
2 × 15 ml spoon (2 tablespoons) chopped fresh parsley, to serve
Dumplings
150 ml (¼ pint) milk
knob of German butter
salt and pepper
pinch of nutmeg
50 g (2 oz) semolina
1 small egg, beaten

Melt the butter in a pan and gently fry the peas for 2–3 minutes. Gradually stir in the flour and then the water. Bring to the boil, stirring all the time. Add the potatoes, mixed herbs and seasoning and simmer for 30 minutes until the vegetables are tender.

Meanwhile, make the dumplings as follows. Heat the milk in the pan with the butter, seasoning and nutmeg. When the milk comes to the boil, remove the pan from the heat and stir in the semolina. Continue stirring until the mixture forms a thick dough. Stir in the egg and scoop out small spoonfuls of the dough. Drop these dumplings into the soup and continue simmering for another 10 minutes. Serve sprinkled with chopped fresh parsley.

CHEESY CHICKEN DRUMSTICKS WITH NOODLES

1 egg, beaten
50 g (2 oz) fresh rye or wholemeal breadcrumbs
25 g (1 oz) Allgäu emmentaler cheese, very finely grated
salt and black pepper
8 large or 12 small chicken drumsticks, skinned
350 g (12 oz) dried spätzle
25 g (1 oz) German butter

Place the beaten egg in a shallow soup bowl. Mix the breadcrumbs, cheese and salt and pepper together in another bowl. Dip the chicken drumsticks first in beaten egg and then in the bread and cheese mixture, making sure they are well coated. Place on a greased baking tray and bake for 45 minutes at 190°C/375°F/Gas Mark 5.

Drop the spätzle into salted boiling water and cook for 10–15 minutes until tender. Drain well and toss in butter. Serve with the chicken.

GERMAN RISOTTO

Use medium-grain or risotto rice, if you can find it, for this dish. Otherwise, use long-grain rice and add just a little less liquid – medium-grain rice is more starchy than long-grain and takes up more liquid.

2 large onions, finely chopped
6 rashers lean smoked bacon, diced
3 × 15 ml spoon (3 tablespoons) cooking oil
175 g (6 oz) German salami or cervelat, skinned and diced
3 large German pickled gherkins, diced
175 g (6 oz) mushrooms, finely chopped
350 g (12 oz) rice
salt and pepper
2 chicken stock cubes
750 ml (1¼ pints) boiling water

Gently fry the onion and bacon in the cooking oil for 3–4 minutes. Add the salami or cervelat, gherkins and mushrooms and continue cooking for a further 3 minutes, stirring all the time. Stir in the rice, making sure that it is well coated with oil, and sprinkle the seasoning over the top. Crumble the stock cubes into the boiling water and pour three-quarters of the liquid over the rice. Bring to the boil, stir and cover. Cook for 14–15 minutes until all the liquid has been absorbed, stirring every 5 minutes or so. Add the rest of the liquid and continue cooking for a further 10 minutes until this, too, has been absorbed. Continue to stir at intervals, taking care not to let the rice stick to the pan as it draws near to the end of the cooking time.

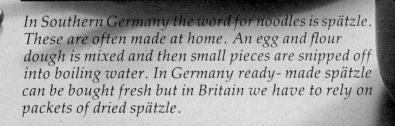

In Southern Germany the word for noodles is spätzle. These are often made at home. An egg and flour dough is mixed and then small pieces are snipped off into boiling water. In Germany ready-made spätzle can be bought fresh but in Britain we have to rely on packets of dried spätzle.

HAMBURGER SPECIAL WITH BEER AND ONION SAUCE

600 g (1¼ lb) minced lean steak
2 × 15 ml spoon (2 tablespoons) tomato ketchup
2 × 15 ml spoon (2 tablespoons) German sweet and sour relish
2 × 15 ml spoon (2 tablespoons) Worcestershire sauce
salt and freshly ground black pepper
cooking oil, for frying
Sauce
1 large onion, finely chopped
15 ml spoon (1 tablespoon) cooking oil
15 g (½ oz) German butter
150 ml (¼ pint) beef stock
1–2 × 5 ml spoon (1–2 teaspoons) gravy thickening
150 ml (¼ pint) German beer
few drops of Tabasco sauce
salt and pepper

Mix all the hamburger ingredients except the cooking oil together in a bowl and shape into four hamburgers. Leave to stand in a cool place for 1 hour.

To make the sauce, fry the onion in the cooking oil until well browned. Stir in the butter. Mix a little of the beef stock with the gravy thickening and add to the pan with the rest of the stock, the beer and Tabasco. Bring to the boil, stirring all the time. Season to taste and simmer for 20 minutes.

Fry the hamburgers in a little more cooking oil for 3–5 minutes on each side, depending on how well cooked you like them. Serve with the sauce and boiled or mashed potatoes.

BRATWURST WITH CURRY SAUCE

Marinate overnight for the best flavour and serve with boiled rice and mango chutney.

8 German bratwurst
300 ml (½ pint) natural yogurt
grated rind and juice of ½ lemon
1 onion, very finely chopped
5 ml spoon (1 teaspoon) fresh root ginger, grated
5 ml spoon (1 teaspoon) curry powder
2 × 5 ml spoon (2 teaspoons) chopped fresh mint *or* 2.5 ml spoon (½ teaspoon) dried mint
salt and pepper
2 × 5 ml spoon (2 teaspoons) cornflour
a little milk

Prick the bratwurst all over with a fork and lay in a long, shallow dish. Mix all the remaining ingredients together except the cornflour and milk and pour over the sausages. Leave in a cool place to marinate for at least 2 hours. Remove the bratwurst from the marinade. Spoon the marinade into a pan. Mix the cornflour and milk and add to the pan. Bring to the boil, stirring all the time, and simmer gently for 5 minutes. Meanwhile, grill the sausages for 2–3 minutes on each side. Serve on a bed of rice with the sauce poured over the top.

In the Nuremburg and Munich areas bratwurst are often cooked over charcoal and served on traditional pewter plates. Pewter may be a little grand for the barbecue but the bratwurst are delicious cooked over the coals.

GREEN BEAN AND SAUSAGE HOTPOT

Large French or runner beans can be used for this recipe.

600 ml (1 pint) chicken stock
1 kg (2 lb) green beans, topped and tailed and with string removed
225 g (8 oz) katenspeck or smoked streaky bacon, diced
2 large onions, chopped
2.5 ml spoon (½ teaspoon) dried savory
40 g (1½ oz) plain flour
salt and pepper
225 g (8 oz) schinkenwurst (German ham sausage) or bierschinken, thickly sliced
knob of German butter

Bring the chicken stock to the boil and add the beans. Cover and simmer for 10–12 minutes until tender. Meanwhile, fry the diced katenspeck or streaky bacon in a large pan with the onion and savory. Stir in the flour and seasoning and then the liquid from the beans. Bring to the boil, stirring from time to time.

Just before the end of the cooking time make small cuts round the outside of each slice of schinkenwurst and fry in a little butter until lightly browned on each side. Spoon the beans into a warmed hotpot dish and arrange the fried sausage over the top. Serve with mashed potato, spätzle or noodles.

STUFFED BREAST OF LAMB MUNICH-STYLE

100 g (4 oz) German liver sausage

1 large onion, finely chopped

1 small green pepper, seeded and finely chopped

salt and pepper

2 large breasts of lamb, boned and skinned

15 ml spoon (1 tablespoon) real German mustard

2 × 15 ml spoon (2 tablespoons) chopped fresh parsley

coarsely ground black pepper

1 packet German potato dumpling mix (optional)

Mix the liver sausage with the onion, green pepper and seasoning and spread over the length of the two breasts. Roll up each one and tie with string. Spread a little mustard all over the outside of each roll. Mix the parsley and black pepper and roll the breasts in the mixture until they are well coated. Place on a baking tray and roast at 190°C/375°F/Gas Mark 5 for 1 hour until cooked through. Meanwhile, make up the potato dumpling mix (if used) as directed on the pack. Slice the lamb and serve with the potato dumplings and vegetables.

SAUSAGE GOULASH

2 onions, sliced

15 ml spoon (1 tablespoon) cooking oil

15 g (½ oz) German butter

1 red pepper, seeded and chopped

1 large green pepper, seeded and chopped

3 tomatoes, chopped

75 ml (3 fl oz) chicken stock

15 ml spoon (1 tablespoon) tomato purée

15 ml spoon (1 tablespoon) paprika pepper

2.5 ml spoon (½ teaspoon) dried marjoram

225 g (8 oz) jagdwurst, schinkenwurst or bierschinken, cut into chunks

3–4 × 15 ml spoon (3–4 tablespoons) soured cream

salt and black pepper

Fry the onions in the cooking oil and butter for 2–3 minutes. Add the peppers and tomatoes and continue frying for a further 2–3 minutes. Pour on the stock and add the tomato purée, paprika and marjoram. Bring to the boil and simmer for 1 hour. Add the sausage, soured cream and gently heat through. Season to taste and serve with spätzle, rice or pasta shapes.

GLAZED HAND OF PORK WITH APPLE SAUERKRAUT

1 hand of pork (approx. 2 kg (4 lb))

3 × 15 ml spoon (3 tablespoons) cherry jam or orange marmalade

75 ml (3 fl oz) German cherry or orange nectar

2–3 × 15 ml spoon (2–3 tablespoons) brown sugar

Apple Sauerkraut

1 small onion, finely sliced

15 g (½ oz) dripping *or* 15 ml spoon (1 tablespoon) cooking oil

450 g (1 lb) can sauerkraut, drained

2 cooking apples, cored and sliced

2.5 ml spoon (½ teaspoon) sugar

10 ml spoon (1 dessertspoon) plain flour

1 potato (approx. 175 g (6 oz)), diced

salt and pepper

pinch of caraway seeds

Place the pork in a roasting tin and roast at 200°C/400°F/Gas Mark 6 for 2 hours. Mix the jam, nectar and sugar in a small pan using a little more sugar with the thinner cherry nectar. Bring to the boil, stirring all the time. Boil for 10 minutes and leave to cool.

Remove the pork from the oven and remove the skin. Brush all over with the fruit glaze and return to the oven for a further 15–20 minutes until well browned.

Meanwhile, fry the onion in dripping or cooking oil until golden. Add the sauerkraut and fry for a further 2 minutes. Barely cover with boiling water and add the apples and sugar. Cover and simmer for 45 minutes. Take a little of the liquid from the pan and mix with the flour to form a smooth, thin paste. Return the mixture to the pan and stir well. Stir in the potato, seasoning and caraway seeds. Cover and cook for a further 10 minutes before serving.

Pictured opposite:
Sausage Goulash
Glazed Hand of Pork with Apple Sauerkraut
Stuffed Breast of Lamb Munich-style

HOT SNACKS AND SUPPER DISHES

FRIED EGG SPECIAL

225 g (8 oz) sliced smoked or German cooked ham, roast beef or cervelat

4 slices German landbrot, lightly buttered

German butter

4 eggs

salt and black pepper

Arrange the slices of ham, beef or cervelat on the bread. Melt the butter in a frying pan and fry the eggs. Place one on top of each slice of bread. Season and serve at once.

BREMEN TOAST

25 g (1 oz) German butter

8 small pork or veal medallions cut from the fillet

juice of ½ lemon

4 small slices German landbrot, toasted

1 × 225 g (8 oz) can asparagus spears

4 slices German ready-sliced cheese

4 tomatoes, halved

Melt the butter in a pan and fry the pork or veal medallions on both sides for 4–5 minutes. Add the lemon juice and toss the medallions in the butter and lemon mixture. Place two medallions and some asparagus on each piece of toast. Cover with a slice of processed cheese and place under a hot grill with the tomatoes. Grill until the cheese begins to bubble and serve at once.

SURPRISE SOUFFLÉD TOAST

225 g (8 oz) peeled prawns
100 g (4 oz) Allgäu emmentaler cheese, grated
2 eggs, separated
salt and pepper
4 slices German landbrot, lightly toasted
2 tomatoes, peeled and sliced

Mix the prawns and cheese with the egg yolks and season to taste. Spread the mixture over the slices of toast and top with tomato slices. Place under the grill and cook for 2–3 minutes. Whisk the egg whites with a little salt until they are very frothy and pile on top of the toast. Place under a lowered grill and cook for 3–4 minutes or until the topping is set and golden.

BALTIC STUFFED POTATOES

This recipe uses matjes herring fillets but you could use chopped rollmop or Bismarck herrings or, for a totally different flavour, smoked mackerel, eel, sealachs or canned saithe.

4 large potatoes, scrubbed and slit with a knife
225 g (8 oz) German quark
100 g (4 oz) German matjes herring fillets, well drained and chopped
3–4 spring onions, chopped, *or* a little chopped onion
black pepper

Bake the potatoes near the top of the oven at 200°C/400°F/Gas Mark 6. They will take about 1–1¼ hours depending on their size.

While the potatoes are cooking mix all the ingredients together and leave to stand for about ½ hour.

Slit the top of the potatoes and open out well. Break up some of the flesh with a fork and spoon the quark and herring mixture over the top. Lightly brown under a hot grill.

In hard times simple dishes were given grand names and Cologne Caviar is still a popular supper dish. It consists of a rye roll filled with blood sausage or black pudding.

SMOKY CHEESE PANCAKES

Both the pancakes and the filling can be made in advance and stored in the freezer. Wrap them separately to freeze. Thaw the pancakes at room temperature and then heat them through in the oven. Thaw the filling in the top of a double pan and put the two together just before serving.

Pancakes

100 g (4 oz) plain flour

pinch of salt

2 eggs

300 ml (½ pint) milk

Filling

2 × 170 g (6 oz) cook-in-the-bag frozen smoked cod or haddock fillets *or* 350 g (12 oz) fresh fish

225 g (8 oz) German camembert or brie with mixed peppers, chopped

75 ml (3 fl oz) single cream

black pepper

Sift the flour and salt into a bowl. Add the eggs and a third of the milk and beat to a smooth paste. Gradually beat in the rest of the milk and leave to stand for 1 hour.

Cook the frozen fish fillets as directed on the pack, or, if using fresh fish, poach it in a little milk until tender. Drain and flake the fish and remove any skin and bones. Place in a pan with the cheese, cream and pepper. Stir over a low heat until creamy and hot.

To make the pancakes, lightly oil a hot griddle or frying pan and pour in sufficient pancake mixture to just cover the base of the pan. Cook until brown underneath, turn over and cook the second side. Continue making pancakes until all the mixture is used up.

Spread each pancake with a little of the fish and cheese mixture and roll up. Serve garnished with wedges of lemon and sprigs of parsley.

SMOKED SAUSAGE AND VEGETABLE TORTILLA

Almost any kind of German smoked sausage, for example cabanos or mettwurst, can be used for this recipe.

25 g (1 oz) German butter

15 ml spoon (1 tablespoon) cooking oil

2 onions, finely chopped

350 g (12 oz) potatoes, peeled and diced

100 g (4 oz) carrots, peeled and diced

3 sticks celery, finely chopped

2 large tomatoes, chopped

2 German smoked sausages (approx. 175 g (6 oz)), diced

salt and pepper

5 eggs, beaten

Melt the butter with the cooking oil in a large frying pan and gently fry the onions for 1–2 minutes. Add the potatoes, carrots, celery and tomatoes and fry gently for 8–10 minutes, stirring from time to time. Stir in the diced sausages and seasoning and pour the beaten eggs over the top. Cook over a slow heat for 15–20 minutes until the base of the tortilla is set and lightly browned. Turn over, in two halves if necessary, and cook the second side for a further 10 minutes. Cut into quarters and serve at once.

CAULIFLOWER AND SAUSAGE AU GRATIN

This recipe is also very good with chicory instead of cauliflower. Use four heads of chicory and cook in just the same way as the cauliflower.

1 cauliflower, broken into florets
50 g (2 oz) German butter
2 × 5 ml spoon (2 teaspoons) lemon juice
4 German frankfurters
25 g (1 oz) plain flour
300 ml (½ pint) milk
75 g (3 oz) Allgäu emmentaler cheese, grated
25 g (1 oz) breadcrumbs made from wholemeal, rye or white bread
salt and pepper

Plunge the cauliflower florets into boiling water. Leave for 5 minutes and drain well. Melt 25 g (1 oz) butter in a frying pan and very gently sauté the florets for 5 minutes, turning from time to time. Add the lemon juice and toss the florets in the butter and lemon mixture. Arrange the cauliflower and frankfurters in the base of a shallow casserole and keep warm.

Melt the remaining butter in a saucepan. Stir in the flour and then the milk and bring to the boil, stirring all the time. Cook for 1–2 minutes. Stir in 50 g (2 oz) cheese and season to taste. Pour over the cauliflower and sausages. Mix the remaining cheese with the breadcrumbs and sprinkle over the top of the dish. Brown under a hot grill.

'HEAVEN AND EARTH' WITH FRANKFURTERS

This is a traditional German dish which takes its name from the way the two main ingredients grow – one on the branches of a tree and one in the earth. How it first got this name it is not known, but whatever the origin of its name this potato–apple mixture goes extremely well with the pork of the frankfurters.

700 g (1½ lb) potatoes, peeled and cubed
800 g (1¾ lb) cooking apples, peeled, cored and sliced
15 ml spoon (1 tablespoon) sugar
5 ml spoon (1 teaspoon) salt
5 ml spoon (1 teaspoon) vinegar
1 onion, finely sliced
100 g (4 oz) katenspeck or streaky bacon, diced
50 g (2 oz) German butter
black pepper
4 long or 8 short German frankfurters

Place the potatoes, apples, sugar, salt and vinegar in a large pan and just cover with water. Bring to the boil and cook for about 15 minutes.

Meanwhile, fry the onion and bacon in half the butter and cook until tender and lightly browned. Keep warm. Heat the frankfurters by leaving them to stand in a pan of very hot water for about 5 minutes.

When the potatoes are cooked, drain them well and mash them. Mix in the remaining butter, season with more salt and black pepper and spoon into a warmed serving dish. Top with the fried onion and bacon mixture and serve with the frankfurters on the side.

At one time only sausages made in the old part of Frankfurt, in the so-called Sausage Quarter, were permitted the name frankfurter. In those days there were 150 specialist butchers all working in one area. However, by the mid nineteenth century frankfurters were being made elsewhere.

SAVOURY SPINACH WITH KNACKWURST

Savoury spinach can be served with almost any kind of 'boiling' sausage. However, knackwurst have a stronger flavour than most and this goes particularly well with the spinach.

1 large onion, finely chopped
50 g (2 oz) German butter
2 × 250 g (9½ oz) packs frozen chopped spinach
1 large 175–225 g (6–8 oz) potato, peeled and grated
salt and black pepper
pinch of nutmeg
8 knackwurst

Fry the onion in butter until lightly browned. Add the spinach, reduce the heat and cover. Leave to thaw for 8–10 minutes, stirring occasionally. Add the potato and seasoning and bring the mixture to the boil. Simmer for 15 minutes. Add the sausages, cover and cook very gently for a further 10 minutes. Serve at once.

SAUSAGE FONDUE

This is great fun for an informal supper party. For eight people, simply double the quantities given below and use two fondue stands.

900 ml (1½ pints) chicken broth (*see recipe for Chicken Soup with Cheese Dumplings on page 16*)
175 g (6 oz) extrawurst or bierwurst, cut into chunks
175 g (6 oz) schinkenwurst or bierschinken, cut into chunks
175 g (6 oz) cervelat, cut into chunks
175 g (6 oz) German cocktail sausages
selection real German mustards
German sweet and sour relish
1 jar baby sweetcorn (maiskölbchen)

Heat the broth in a pan in the kitchen and transfer it to the fondue pan. Keep just below simmering point over the flame. Arrange a portion of each kind of sausage on the fondue plates. Serve two or three kinds of mustard, relish and sweetcorn on side dishes. Each person spears a piece of sausage and warms it through in the fondue pan, and the baby sweetcorn may be treated in the same way.
Pictured opposite

BAKED HUNTER'S CABBAGE

This quick-to-prepare recipe makes an excellent supper dish. Serve with jacket potatoes and tomato ketchup.

100 g (4 oz) katenspeck or streaky bacon, diced
1 large onion, sliced
15 ml spoon (1 tablespoon) cooking oil
350 g (12 oz) white cabbage, shredded
1 large cooking apple, peeled, cored and sliced
salt and black pepper
6–8 juniper berries
3 × 15 ml spoon (3 tablespoons) German dry white wine, cider or stock
4–6 large bockwurst

Fry the katenspeck or bacon and onion in cooking oil in a large frying pan. After 3–4 minutes stir in the shredded cabbage and continue frying gently for a further 3–4 minutes, stirring all the time. Add all the remaining ingredients and bring to the boil. Transfer to a casserole dish. Cover and bake at 190°C/375°F/Gas Mark 5 for 45 minutes. Cut the sausages in half and add to the casserole. Toss in the cabbage mixture and return to the oven for 10 minutes to heat through.

WINTER WARMERS

WHITE BEAN SOUP WITH SMOKED SAUSAGE

Almost any kind of well-flavoured German smoked sausage can be used in this soup. Serve as it is for a coarsely textured soup or remove the sausage, purée the soup and then return the sausage to the mixture. Reheat and serve.

2 onions, chopped
15 ml spoon (1 tablespoon) cooking oil
15 ml spoon (1 tablespoon) plain flour
100 g (4 oz) large or small haricot beans, soaked overnight in cold water and then drained
600 ml (1 pint) chicken stock
1 × 400 g (14 oz) can tomatoes
225 g (8 oz) jagdwurst, German salami or schinkenwurst, skinned but not sliced
2.5 ml spoon (½ teaspoon) dried thyme
salt and freshly ground black pepper

Fry the onions in cooking oil until lightly browned. Stir in the flour and then the beans. Gradually stir in the stock, bring to the boil and simmer for 2–3 minutes. Add the contents of the can of tomatoes, the piece of sausage, herbs and seasoning. Cover and simmer for 1½ hours until the beans are tender. Remove the sausage, slice or chop and return to the soup.

BROWN KIDNEY SOUP WITH FRIED BREAD CROÛTONS

1 onion, chopped
2 × 15 ml spoon (2 tablespoons) cooking oil
1 large leek, sliced
1 large carrot, chopped
1 turnip or small swede, chopped
225 g (8 oz) ox kidney, chopped with the core removed
5 ml spoon (1 teaspoon) real German mustard
1 bay leaf
salt and pepper
1 litre (1¾ pints) beef stock
Croûtons
2 slices fresh German landbrot
50 g (2 oz) German butter
2–3 slices German processed cheese

Fry the onion in cooking oil for 2–3 minutes. Add the remaining vegetables and fry gently for a further 3–4 minutes. Next add the kidney, mustard, bay leaf and seasoning. Stir well to seal the kidney and then add the stock. Bring to the boil. Cover and simmer for 1 hour.

Remove the bay leaf and, if you like a smooth soup, rub the cooked vegetables through a sieve or process the soup in a blender. Return to the pan to reheat. Meanwhile, fry the bread in butter until golden on both sides. Remove from the pan and cover with sliced processed cheese and place under the grill until the cheese bubbles. Remove from the grill and leave to cool. Cut into squares and use to garnish the soup.

SAUSAGE AND POTATO CHOWDER

The delicate flavours of the leeks and potatoes need a fairly mild sausage to complement them. Try this recipe with bierwurst or extrawurst. It is also very good with the lean part of katenspeck if you can find it.

2 large onions, sliced
4 large leeks, sliced
1.25 ml spoon (¼ teaspoon) caraway seeds
25 g (1 oz) German butter
1 kg (2 lb) potatoes, diced
900 ml (1½ pints) chicken stock
salt and freshly ground black pepper
225 g (8 oz) mild German sausage, diced
4 × 15 ml spoon (4 tablespoons) soured cream
1.25 ml spoon (¼ teaspoon) nutmeg

Fry the onions, leeks and caraway seeds in butter for 3–4 minutes. Add the potatoes, stock and seasoning. Bring to the boil, cover and simmer for 45 minutes. Add the remaining ingredients and heat through. Serve as a main course soup with plenty of bread or serve smaller helpings as a starter and keep the rest for another day.

GERMAN BRIE AND ONION SOUP

This is a wonderfully warming soup for winter days. It can be made with any of the different flavours of German brie cheese. Serve with big hunks of rye bread or sprinkle with fried bread croûtons.

40 g (1½ oz) German butter
1 onion, finely chopped
25 g (1 oz) plain flour
300 ml (½ pint) chicken stock
300 ml (½ pint) milk
75 g (3 oz) German brie (mushroom, green pepper or blue)
salt and pepper

Melt half the butter in a saucepan and fry the onion until very lightly browned. Remove the onion from the pan and keep on one side. Add the rest of the butter to the pan. When it has melted, stir in the flour and then the stock and milk. Bring to the boil, stirring all the time. Remove the rind from the cheese and cut into small pieces. Add these to the soup and stir until they have melted. Add the onion and season to taste. Pour into individual bowls to serve.

BEEF AND BEER STEW WITH DUMPLINGS

75 g (3 oz) streaky bacon, diced

2 large onions, chopped

6 peppercorns

2 × 15 ml spoon (2 tablespoons) cooking oil

2 carrots, chopped

2 sticks celery, chopped

900 g (2 lb) chuck steak, cubed

1 × 220 g (7½ oz) can prunes

275 ml (12 fl oz) German beer

5 ml spoon (1 teaspoon) real German mustard

5 ml spoon (1 teaspoon) sugar

salt and pepper

Dumplings

100 g (4 oz) stale German landbrot

75 ml (3 fl oz) hot milk

15 g (½ oz) German butter

1 very small onion, finely chopped

15 ml spoon (1 tablespoon) chopped fresh parsley

1 egg, beaten

pinch of nutmeg

25 g (1 oz) plain flour

salt and pepper

Fry the bacon, onions and peppercorns in cooking oil for 2–3 minutes. Add the carrots and celery and the meat and continue frying until the meat is well sealed. Add the rest of the stew ingredients, bring to the boil and simmer for 2 hours, stirring from time to time.

Meanwhile, make the dumplings. Soak the bread in hot milk for 1 hour. Melt the butter and fry the onion until lightly browned, and then stir the onion into the bread and milk with the parsley, beaten egg and nutmeg. Mix in the flour and season. Shape into eight small dumplings and poach in simmering water for 10–15 minutes. Serve on top of the stew.

BREMEN LOBSCOUSE

1 kg (2 lb) potatoes, peeled and quartered

salt and pepper

2 onions, finely chopped

25 g (1 oz) German butter

3–4 × 15 ml spoon (3–4 tablespoons) hot beef stock

350 g (12 oz) cooked brisket of beef, salt beef or corned beef, chopped

pinch of nutmeg

pinch of sugar

2–3 German matjes herring fillets (150 g (5 oz) pack, drained), chopped

2 small beetroot, cooked and diced

4 German pickled gherkins, sliced

4 eggs, fried

Cook the potatoes in salted water until tender. Meanwhile, fry the onion in butter until just tender. Drain and mash the potatoes and mix in the onion and sufficient beef stock to make the mixture light and fluffy. Next, stir in the meat and heat through thoroughly. Add the nutmeg and sugar and check the seasoning. Pile the mixture on to four warmed plates and surround with piles of chopped matjes herrings, diced beetroot and sliced gherkin. Alternatively, mix all these ingredients together. Top each pile with a fried egg and serve at once.

In the northern coastal parts of Germany the combination of meat and fish in the same dish is quite common. German Labskaus or Seaman's Hash is one such dish. It is traditionally made with salt beef and matjes herrings, and served with potatoes and pickles.

STUFFED CABBAGE LEAVES

8 or 16 large cabbage leaves
Filling
75 g (3 oz) rice
2 onions, finely chopped
15 ml spoon (1 tablespoon) cooking oil
150 g (5 oz) German liver sausage
25 g (1 oz) raisins
25 g (1 oz) almonds
200 g (7 oz) German quark
2.5 ml spoon (½ teaspoon) mixed herbs
pinch of caraway seeds
salt and pepper
Sauce
450 ml (¾ pint) tomato juice
2–3 × 15 ml spoon (2–3 tablespoons) soured cream

Blanch the cabbage leaves by plunging them into salted boiling water for 5 minutes and then drain them. Cook the rice in 175 ml (6 fl oz) salted boiling water for 12 minutes until all the water has been absorbed and the rice is tender.

Fry the onions in cooking oil until lightly browned. Mix with the rice and stir in the liver sausage, quark, raisins and almonds. Add sufficient tomato juice to give a thick but soft consistency and stir in the herbs, caraway seeds and seasonings. Divide the mixture up into 8 or 16 portions according to the number of cabbage leaves used, and parcel up each portion in a cabbage leaf. Place the parcels in a shallow ovenproof dish and pour on the rest of the tomato juice and the soured cream. Cover and bake at 180°C/350°F/Gas Mark 4 for 45–50 minutes.

There are around 1500 different breweries in Germany all brewing their own beer – more than 5000 varieties in all – and between them producing 1760 million gallons of beer every year! It has been calculated that the average German drinks 255 pints every year compared with 214 pints for the average Briton.

SAUSAGE PASTA PIE

6–8 pieces lasagne
salt
2 onions, chopped
2 × 15 ml spoon (2 tablespoons) cooking oil
1 green pepper, seeded and chopped
100 g (4 oz) button mushrooms, chopped
1 × 425 g (15 oz) can tomatoes
salt and pepper
2.5 ml spoon (½ teaspoon) dried oregano
50 g (2 oz) German butter
50 g (2 oz) plain flour
600 ml (1 pint) milk
175 g (6 oz) Allgäu emmentaler cheese, grated
175 g (6 oz) bierwurst or bierschinken, sliced

Cook the lasagne in salted water as directed on the pack. Drain and keep on one side. Fry the onion in cooking oil for 2–3 minutes. Add the green pepper and mushrooms and continue cooking for a further 2–3 minutes. Add the contents of the can of tomatoes, seasoning and oregano. Bring the mixture to the boil and simmer for 15 minutes.

Melt the butter in a pan and stir in the flour. Gradually add the milk and bring to the boil, stirring all the time. Cook for a minute or two and then stir in two-thirds of the cheese and season to taste. Layer the lasagne, sausage slices, tomato sauce and cheese sauce in a shallow ovenproof dish. Finish with a layer of cheese sauce and sprinkle the remaining cheese on top. Bake at 190°C/375°F/Gas Mark 5 for 30 minutes.

Pictured below

BRAISED KNUCKLE OF PORK WITH APPLES

4 small pork knuckles
4 onions, sliced
3 carrots, sliced
3 × 15 ml spoon (3 tablespoons) vinegar
1 bay leaf
1 clove
25 g (1 oz) German butter, melted
3 cooking apples, peeled, cored and cut into thick slices
150 ml (¼ pint) German apple juice
15 ml spoon (1 tablespoon) cranberry jelly (optional)

Place the pork knuckles in a large saucepan with the onions, carrots, vinegar, bay leaf and clove. Cover with water and bring to the boil. Cover and simmer very gently for 45 minutes. Drain the meat, retaining the vegetables, bay leaf and clove. Brush the meat with butter and place in a large braising dish. Add the vegetables, herbs, apple slices and apple juice. Cover and bake at 180°C/350°F/Gas Mark 4 for about 2 hours until the pork is very tender. Serve with the vegetables and a little of the cooking liquor (which may be mixed with cranberry jelly, reheated and poured over the meat), and potatoes or potato dumplings and red cabbage.

GERMAN BEANPOT WITH SMOKED SAUSAGE AND SPECK

Use smoked streaky bacon for this dish if you cannot find any kind of speck.

75 g (3 oz) speck or katenspeck, diced
2 onions, finely chopped
100 g (4 oz) jagdwurst or schinkenwurst, diced
50 g (2 oz) German salami, diced
salt and pepper
100 g (4 oz) haricot beans (*or* 50 g (2 oz) each of haricot beans and black eye beans), soaked overnight in cold water and then drained
50 g (2 oz) butter beans, soaked overnight in cold water and then drained
150 ml (¼ pint) German wine or cider
chicken stock

Fry the speck or katenspeck to release some of the fat. Add the onions and continue frying until the onions are lightly browned. Add the diced sausages and seasoning. Mix the beans together and layer the beans and onions and sausage mixture in a small but deep earthenware casserole. Pour on the wine or cider and add sufficient stock for the liquid to come three-quarters of the way up the beans. Cover and bake at 170°C/325°F/Gas Mark 3 for 3–4 hours until most of the liquid has been taken up.

Pictured opposite:
German Beanpot with Smoked Sausage and Speck
Braised Knuckle of Pork with Apples

SALADS AND COLD COOKERY

APPLESLAW

This is a really refreshing salad which goes well with barbecues and grills. Use sauerkraut instead of white cabbage for a change of flavour and texture.

1 eating apple, coarsely grated

5 ml spoon (1 teaspoon) lemon juice

1 large carrot, coarsely grated

225 g (8 oz) white cabbage, finely shredded

2 × 15 ml spoon (2 tablespoons) German quark

1–2 × 15 ml spoon (1–2 tablespoons) German apple juice

black pepper

Mix the apple with the lemon juice to prevent discolouring. Add the carrot and cabbage and mix well together. Mix the quark and apple juice to a thin, smooth cream and pour over the salad. Season with black pepper.

MIXED GREEN SALAD WITH BLUE CHEESE DRESSING

1 small lettuce, washed

5 cm (2 in) cucumber, thinly sliced

½ bunch watercress, washed, *or* ½ head curly endive, washed and chopped

Dressing

100 g (4 oz) German quark

25 g (1 oz) pilzkäse, crumbled

2 × 5 ml spoon (2 teaspoons) wine or cider vinegar

pepper

Tear the lettuce into small pieces and place in a salad bowl with the cucumber and watercress or endive. Mix the quark and pilzkäse with a fork, mashing the two well together, and add the vinegar and sufficient water to give a thin but creamy consistency. Alternatively, process in a blender, adding the water a little at a time until the right consistency is reached. Season to taste with black peper and pour over the salad. Toss all together just before serving.

SPICY HERRING SALAD

Matjes herrings are the best kind of herring to use in this recipe, but Bismarck or rollmop herrings could be used instead. Add potatoes for a more substantial salad.

100 g (4 oz) German matjes herrings, cut into strips
1 small onion, grated or very finely chopped
2 eggs, hard-boiled and chopped
150 ml (¼ pint) soured cream
2 × 5 ml spoon (2 teaspoons) lemon juice
salt and pepper
paprika pepper
225 g (8 oz) cold boiled potatoes, diced (optional)
1 egg, hard-boiled and quartered, to garnish

Place all the ingredients in a bowl and mix well together. You may need to add a little milk if the cream is very thick. Leave to stand in a cool place for an hour or so before using. Garnish with hard-boiled egg and serve with German landbrot.

POTATO SALAD

This recipe uses paprika-flavoured dressing, but any of the creamy German bottled dressings would be suitable. Serve with a cold meat or sausage platter or mix in the optional cheese and serve as a supper dish with a green salad and tomatoes. This salad can also be made with extrawurst in place of the cheese. The former is traditional in the North and the latter in the South.

600 g (1¼ lb) potatoes
salt
8 spring onions, very finely chopped
1 small dill pickled cucumber or large gherkin, very finely chopped
3 × 15 ml spoon (3 tablespoons) German paprika-flavoured dressing (or mayonnaise mixed with paprika pepper)
black pepper
175 g (6 oz) German tilsiter cheese, diced (optional)
sprigs of parsley or watercress, to garnish

Boil the potatoes in their skins in salted water until tender. Take care not to overcook them or the skins will split and the potatoes will break up. Peel the potatoes and leave them to cool. Dice the peeled potatoes and mix with all the remaining ingredients. Spoon into a serving bowl and garnish with sprigs of parsley or watercress.

In Germany there are no less than 1500 different kinds of sausage to choose from and not surprisingly they are a favourite for the lighter evening meal. They may be served with salads, on their own with bread or hot with potato salad and they are just as likely to appear at breakfast as at supper!

EGG AND HERRING FLAN

175 g (6 oz) shortcrust pastry

3 × 150 g (5 oz) packs German matjes herrings, well drained and chopped

2 eggs, hard-boiled and sliced

2 × 15 ml spoon (2 tablespoons) capers

1 × 25 g (1 oz) packet aspic

Roll out the pastry and use to line a 20 cm (8 in) loose-based flan case. Prick the base of the flan with a fork and bake blind at 190°C/375°F/Gas Mark 5 for 20 minutes until crisp and golden. Leave to cool. Remove from the flan case and place on a flat plate. Fill with chopped herrings and slices of egg, and sprinkle the capers on the top of the flan. Make up the aspic as directed on the pack and leave to cool. Pour over the flan and leave in a cool place to set.

SLIMMERS' SAUERKRAUT SALAD

450 g (1 lb) German wine sauerkraut

225 g (8 oz) German quark

1 grapefruit, peeled and segmented

1 cooking apple, grated

1 small onion, finely chopped

1 small lettuce

Mix the sauerkraut with the quark, grapefruit and apple, and then mix in the onion to taste. Serve on a bed of lettuce.

Pictured below

PRESSED CHEESE AND SAUSAGE LOAF

225 g (8 oz) carrots, grated

100 g (4 oz) Allgäu emmentaler or bergkäse, grated

100 g (4 oz) German tilsiter cheese, grated

4 × 15 ml spoon (4 tablespoons) mayonnaise

black pepper

100 g (4 oz) extrawurst or bierwurst, finely chopped

5 ml spoon (1 teaspoon) real German mustard

2 large German pickled gherkins, finely chopped

shredded lettuce, to decorate

Mix the carrots, cheeses and mayonnaise in a bowl and season with pepper. Mix the sausage, gherkins and mustard together in another bowl and season to taste. Press the carrot and cheese mixture into a 450 g (1 lb) loaf tin and hollow out the centre. Spoon in the sausage and gherkin mixture and push well down. Chill for at least 1 hour. Turn out and decorate with shredded lettuce. Serve in slices.

STUFFED SLICED SAUSAGE ROLLS SET IN ASPIC

1 × 25 g (1 oz) packet aspic

75 g (3 oz) extrawurst or bierwurst 10 cm (4 in) in diameter, sliced

Fillings

100 g (4 oz) German tilsiter cheese, grated

1 carrot, grated

15 ml spoon (1 tablespoon) German quark

2.5 ml spoon (½ teaspoon) celery salt

black pepper

or

2 eggs, hard-boiled and finely chopped

50 g (2 oz) peeled prawns, chopped

15 ml spoon (1 tablespoon) mayonnaise

salt and black pepper

and

75 g (3 oz) peas, cooked

watercress, to garnish

Make up the aspic as directed on the pack and leave to cool. Mix together the chosen filling ingredients and spread a quarter of the mixture over each slice of sausage. Roll up and secure with half a cocktail stick. Press a few peas into each end. Place in a shallow dish just large enough to take the rolls. Cover with aspic and leave in the fridge to set. Turn out to serve. Garnish with watercress.

Pictured opposite:
Egg and Herring Flan
Pressed Cheese and Sausage Loaf
Stuffed Sliced Sausage Rolls set in Aspic

SIMPLE SAUSAGE SALAD

4 long German frankfurters or bockwurst (350 g (12 oz))

4 German pickled gherkins (100 g (4 oz))

1 bunch radishes

4 sticks celery, sliced

3 green eating apples, cored and diced

100 g (4 oz) Allgäu emmentaler cheese, diced

3 tomatoes, skinned and diced

3 × 15 ml spoon (3 tablespoons) salad oil

15 ml spoon (1 tablespoon) cider or wine vinegar

2.5 ml spoon (½ teaspoon) real German mustard (optional)

5 ml spoon (1 teaspoon) dried chervil

1.25 ml spoon (¼ teaspoon) dried dill

black pepper

Slice the sausages, gherkins and radishes into thin rounds and mix in a bowl with the celery, apple, cheese and tomatoes. Mix all the remaining ingredients together and pour over the salad.

GRAPEFRUIT AND SALAMI COCKTAIL

Almost any kind of German salami or firm smoked sausage can be used for this recipe. For a change try using quark in place of mayonnaise. Serve with other salads or as a starter.

2 grapefruit
100 g (4 oz) German salami, in one piece
1 large German pickled gherkin, finely diced
2 × 15 ml spoon (2 tablespoons) thick mayonnaise
salt and pepper
sprigs of mint or parsley, to decorate

Cut the grapefruit in half and scoop or cut out all the flesh. Reserve the halves. Remove any pith, pips or thick membranes and chop finely. Skin the piece of salami and cut into fine dice. Mix the grapefruit and salami with the diced gherkin and mayonnaise and season to taste. Pile the mixture back into the grapefruit halves and decorate with sprigs of mint or parsley.

CHICORY AND CHEESE SALAD WITH BEETROOT

This makes an excellent main course salad. Alternatively it can be served as part of a cold buffet. Choose any firm cheese and substitute shallots or a small onion when spring onions are out of season.

2 heads chicory (approx. 225 g (8 oz)), sliced
6 spring onions, finely chopped
175 g (6 oz) Allgäu emmentaler cheese, diced
2 × 15 ml spoon (2 tablespoons) German quark
2 × 15 ml spoon (2 tablespoons) mayonnaise
5 ml spoon (1 teaspoon) lemon juice
black pepper
2 medium beetroot, cooked and diced

Put the chicory, onion and cheese together in a bowl. Add the quark, mayonnaise and lemon juice and mix well together. Season to taste with black pepper. Stir in the beetroot just before serving.

VEGETABLE MEDLEY

SAUERKRAUT WITH SAUSAGES AND PEPPERS

Use sauerkraut direct from the can or jar. Drain it but do not wash it.

1 large onion, chopped
25 g (1 oz) lard or dripping *or* 2 × 15 ml spoon (2 tablespoons) cooking oil
½ green pepper, seeded and diced
335 g (11½ oz) jar German sauerkraut
50 g (2 oz) German salami or cervelat, very finely diced
1 bay leaf
300 ml (½ pint) beef stock
5 ml spoon (1 teaspoon) sugar
100 g (4 oz) potato, grated
black pepper

Fry the onion in lard, dripping or cooking oil until well browned. Add the green pepper and fry for a further minute or two. Add all the remaining ingredients except the potato and black pepper. Bring the mixture to the boil. Cover and simmer for 45 minutes.

Add the potatoes and pepper and continue cooking for another 15 minutes. Stir well and serve with grilled or boiled sausages, such as bratwurst or German frankfurters, or pot-roasted meats.

LEEKS WITH BLUE CHEESE SAUCE

This is a firm favourite both as an accompaniment to roasts and grills and as a starter to a special dinner. In the latter case, serve in individual ramekin dishes with crusty brown rolls.

8–10 leeks, trimmed and cut into short lengths
50 g (2 oz) German butter
50 g (2 oz) plain flour
450 ml (¾ pint) milk
100 g (4 oz) German blue brie or pilzkäse
salt and pepper
25 g (1 oz) fresh brown breadcrumbs

Steam the leeks or boil in a very little water for 10–12 minutes until tender.

Melt the butter in a pan and stir in the flour. Gradually add the milk and bring the mixture to the boil, stirring all the time. Add a little of the cooking liquor from the leeks if the sauce seems too thick. Stir in the cheese and season. Use the salt sparingly with pilzkäse as it can taste very salty.

Arrange the leeks in a heatproof serving dish or in individual ramekin dishes and pour the sauce over the top. Sprinkle with breadcrumbs and brown under the grill. Serve at once.

FRANCONIAN SAUERKRAUT

This recipe was given to me by one of my very helpful guides on a recent visit to Germany and very good it is too. It is best made the day before it is wanted and reheated before eating.

1 large onion, finely chopped
25 g (1 oz) German butter
335 g (11½ oz) jar German sauerkraut
5 ml spoon (1 teaspoon) juniper berries
1.25 ml spoon (¼ teaspoon) caraway seeds
1 bay leaf
4 × 15 ml spoon (4 tablespoons) German wine
300 ml (½ pint) good chicken stock

Fry the onion in butter until lightly browned. Add all the remaining ingredients and bring to the boil. Cover and simmer for 45 minutes. Leave to cool.

The next day bring the mixture back to the boil and simmer for a further 20 minutes. Serve with grilled frankfurters.

Sauerkraut is salted cabbage. The cabbage is placed in wooden barrels with salt and left to ferment for several weeks. All kinds of things may be used to flavour sauerkraut and these include beer, wine, juniper berries, apples, cloves, peppercorns and onions. Sauerkraut is usually sold in jars or cans and provided that it is not opened it will keep almost for ever!

LEEKS AND PEAS WITH SALAMI AND CREAM

The little pieces of salami add an unusual touch to this dish of creamed leeks and peas. Serve it with plain roasts and grills for the best effect.

25 g (1 oz) German butter
700 g (1½ lb) leeks, trimmed and sliced
225 g (8 oz) fresh or frozen peas
50 g (2 oz) German salami, skinned
4 × 15 ml spoon (4 tablespoons) double cream
salt and pepper

Melt the butter in a saucepan. Add the leeks and very gently fry for 6–8 minutes. Stir from time to time and do not allow the leeks to brown. Add the peas and 15 ml spoon (1 tablespoon) water if fresh peas are used. Continue to cook the vegetables over a low heat for a further 8 minutes until both are tender. Cut the salami into very small dice and add to the pan with the cream and seasoning. Toss over the heat until warmed through and turn into a serving dish.

In Northern Germany potatoes are served in just the same way as in the UK but in Southern Germany they are much more likely to turn up as dumplings. The classic recipe uses two-thirds grated raw potato to one-third boiled potato, but recipes vary from family to family. Dumplings are quite difficult to make if you do not have the knack but you can buy packet mixes of potato dumplings which take much of the guesswork out of making them.

GERMAN-STYLE SAUTÉ POTATOES

The katenspeck gives a really distinctive and delicious flavour to this simple dish of fried potatoes. However, if you cannot find any katenspeck use smoked streaky bacon instead.

1 kg (2 lb) potatoes

175 g (6 oz) katenspeck, diced

1 small onion, very finely chopped

salt and pepper

Parboil the potatoes in their skins in lightly salted water for 7–8 minutes. They should still be very firm. Leave to cool a little and peel. Cut the potatoes into thin irregularly shaped slices and keep on one side. Fry the diced katenspeck in a large frying pan to release some of the fat. Add the onion and continue frying for a minute or two. Next, add the potatoes and fry for 8–10 minutes, turning from time to time.

One of my favourite accompaniments to a good many dishes is this German version of sauté potatoes (called rostkartoffeln). The katenspeck seems to give the potatoes quite a different flavour from sautéing in butter or oil. Serve with hot sausages, roast meats, omelettes or fried chicken.

CREAMY POTATO HOTPOT WITH ONIONS AND SPECK

The white speck imparts its own special flavour to the onion in this dish and the brie melts into the casserole to give a really creamy texture. If you cannot get speck, use butter or dripping.

25 g (1 oz) white speck, cut into very small dice

1 large onion, sliced

75 g (3 oz) German herb brie

600 g (1¼ lb) potatoes, peeled and sliced

salt and pepper

150 ml (¼ pint) milk

Fry the white speck in a frying pan to release some of the fat and fry the onion in this until lightly browned. Remove the rind from the brie and slice. Layer the potatoes in a small casserole dish with the fried onions and cheese and season as you go. End with a layer of potato. Pour in the milk, cover and bake at 190°C/375°F/Gas Mark 5 for 1 hour. Remove the lid and brown if necessary.

BEAN BUNDLES

If you cannot find katenspeck, use thin strips of German smoked ham or smoked streaky bacon.

350 g (12 oz) small French beans
4 thin slices katenspeck
salt and freshly ground black pepper

Top and tail the beans and arrange them in four bundles. Wrap a slice of speck round each bundle and secure with a cocktail stick. Place in a steamer over gently boiling water. Cover and steam for 10–15 minutes until the beans are tender. Arrange on a serving dish and sprinkle with a little salt and black pepper.

Pictured below

BAKED SAVOURY RICE WITH SPÄTZLE

This is an excellent way of cooking rice when you have the oven on for another dish. The spätzle give a different texture to the dish. If you cannot find any, use spaghetti instead.

1 small onion, finely chopped
½ green pepper, finely chopped
15 g (½ oz) German butter
2 × 15 ml spoon (2 tablespoons) cooking oil
175 g (6 oz) long-grain rice
50 g (2 oz) spätzle, broken into small pieces
1 × 290 g (10½ oz) can condensed consommé
175 ml (6 fl oz) water
salt and black pepper

Fry the onion and green pepper in butter and oil for 3–4 minutes until softened. Stir in the rice and the spätzle and thoroughly coat with fat. Transfer to a casserole dish. Mix together the consommé and water and bring to the boil, pour over the rice mixture, season and stir once. Cover with a lid and bake at 180°C/350°F/Gas Mark 4 for 45–50 minutes until all the liquid has been absorbed. Fluff up with a fork before serving.

STIR-FRIED MIXED VEGETABLES WITH SALAMI

25 g (1 oz) German butter
15 ml spoon (1 tablespoon) cooking oil
2 × 300 g (10 oz) packets frozen stir-fry mixed vegetables
50 g (2 oz) German salami or cervelat, skinned and diced

Heat the butter and oil in a frying pan or wok and toss in the vegetables and salami. Stir-fry over a good heat for 3–4 minutes until the vegetables are crisp but tender.

Pictured opposite:
Baked Savoury Rice with Spätzle
Stir-fried Mixed Vegetables with Salami

SANDWICHES AND PACKED LUNCHES

MAINZ MONARCH

1 large onion, finely chopped

15 ml spoon (1 tablespoon) cooking oil

German butter

4 slices German landbrot (fresh or toasted) or leinsamenbrot

350 g (12 oz) coarse or smooth German liver sausage

4 large German pickled gherkins, cut into fans

4 tomatoes, sliced

Fry the onion in cooking oil until well browned and leave to cool. Butter the landbrot or leinsamenbrot. Cut the liver sausage into 12 thick slices. Arrange three overlapping slices on each piece of bread. Sprinkle the top with fried onions and arrange a sliced tomato and a gherkin fan on each side.

PINT AND PARTNER

Almost any kind of German slicing sausage could be used in this recipe but I have chosen bierwurst as it goes so well with cheese and beer.

4 lettuce leaves

4 rounds German landbrot, buttered

175 g (6 oz) (8–12 slices) bierwurst

100 g (4 oz) German tilsiter cheese, cut into strips

2 tomatoes, cut into flowers

4 × 5 ml spoon (4 teaspoons) German sweet and sour relish or other pickle

Arrange the lettuce leaves at one end of each slice of bread. Fold the slices of bierwurst and place on the lettuce. Arrange the cheese on the remaining space. Garnish each sandwich with a tomato flower and about 5 ml spoon (1 teaspoon) relish. Serve with foaming glasses of German beer.

Often known as the Oktoberfest, even though it usually takes place in September, the Munich Beer Festival lasts for two weeks. The festival is held in huge tents in the Therese Meadows in Munich. The festival was founded on the occasion of the wedding of Crown Prince Ludwig of Bavaria to the Princess Therese, after whom the meadows are named.

BALTIC BRUNCH

225 g (8 oz) smoked fish (mackerel, buckling, sprats, trout or eel)

4 rounds German landbrot, buttered

4 lettuce leaves

225 g (8 oz) can potato salad

2 × 15 ml spoon (2 tablespoons) apple sauce or purée

2 × 15 ml spoon (2 tablespoons) creamed horseradish

1 tomato, sliced

8 pickled baby sweetcorn (maiskölbchen)

4 thin slices lemon

Skin and bone whole fish or drain canned fish. Cut into strips and arrange at one end of each round of bread. Place a lettuce leaf at the other end and top with a spoonful of potato salad. Mix together the apple and horseradish. Garnish the salad with a slice of tomato and a spoonful of apple–horseradish mixture and garnish the fish with two pickled sweetcorn and a twist of lemon.

MATJES MAJOR

4 rounds German landbrot or vollkornbrot, buttered

4 × 10 ml spoon (4 dessertspoons) apple purée or sauce

4 × 5 ml spoon (4 teaspoons) cranberry sauce

100 g (4 oz) German matjes herrings, sliced

2 eggs, hard-boiled and sliced

2 × 15 ml spoon (2 tablespoons) mayonnaise mixed with 2.5 ml spoon (½ teaspoon) curry powder

1 canned pimento, cut into strips, or ¼ green pepper, seeded and cut into strips

Place 10 ml spoon (1 dessertspoon) apple purée or sauce at one end of the slice of bread and 5 ml spoon (1 teaspoon) of cranberry sauce next to it. Arrange the sliced herring fillets in the middle of the bread and place the sliced egg at the other end. Top with curry mayonnaise and decorate with strips of pimento or green pepper.

RYE DECKERS

This mixture of dark pumpernickel and white bread looks very attractive with the contrasting colours of the fillings. The sandwiches can be made in the morning and placed in a rigid container or wrapped in foil and kept in the fridge until required.

LIVER AND LETTUCE

Makes 16 small sandwiches

8 slices white bread

4 slices pumpernickel

25 g (1 oz) German butter, softened

175 g (6 oz) German liver sausage

black pepper

2 × 15 ml spoon (2 tablespoons) German mixed vegetable relish

75 g (3 oz) lettuce leaves, shredded

Cut the white bread to the same size as the pumpernickel, removing all the crusts in the process. Butter all the slices of bread and spread half the white slices with liver sausage. Season with black pepper. Mix the relish and lettuce leaves and press on to the slices of pumpernickel. Place each slice of pumpernickel on top of the liver sausage slices and top with another slice of white bread. Cut each double-decker sandwich into four small sandwiches. Leinsamenbrot also tastes good in this recipe for a change.

HERRING AND BEETROOT

Makes 16 small sandwiches

8 slices white bread

4 slices pumpernickel

25 g (1 oz) German butter, softened

2 smoked herring or buckling

2 × 5 ml spoon (2 teaspoons) mild horseradish cream

a little lemon juice

black pepper

100 g (4 oz) cooked beetroot, grated

50 g (2 oz) German dill gherkins, finely chopped

1–2 × 5 ml spoon (1–2 teaspoons) mayonnaise

Cut the white bread to the same size as the pumpernickel, removing all the crusts in the process. Butter all the slices of bread. Skin the fish and remove all the bones. Mash the flesh with the horseradish cream and a little lemon juice and black pepper. Spread on half the slices of white bread. Mix the grated beetroot, chopped dill gherkin and mayonnaise and spread over the slices of pumpernickel. Place the slices of pumpernickel on top of the herring and top with another slice of white bread. Cut each double-decker sandwich into four small sandwiches.

ROLL-UPS

Really fresh brown bread is the best choice for these sandwiches. If the bread is difficult to cut, dip the bread knife into a tall jug of boiling water between each cut. Use different cheeses or German liver sausage for a change.

SMOKY CHEESE

8 slices large fresh brown tin loaf

25 g (1 oz) German butter

300 g (10 oz) German smoked cheese, grated

2 × 15 ml spoon (2 tablespoons) German paprika-flavoured dressing (*or* mayonnaise mixed with paprika pepper)

Butter the bread and remove the crusts. Mix the smoked cheese and salad dressing or mayonnaise and spread over each slice of bread. Roll up like a Swiss roll.

SPICY SAUSAGE

8 slices large fresh brown tin loaf

25 g (1 oz) German butter

300 g (10 oz) teewurst (2 small sausages)

4 × 15 ml spoon (4 tablespoons) chopped fresh parsley

Butter the bread and remove the crusts. Mix the teewurst and parsley and spread a portion over each slice of bread. Roll up like a Swiss roll.

Despite many changes in the food available and in eating habits generally, one custom has remained unchanged in Germany: unlike in Britain, the main meal of the day is still eaten at midday. This meal will usually consist of soup followed by meat and vegetables, and may be finished off with a sweet dessert or with fruit.

Pictured opposite:
Roll-ups: Smoky Cheese, Spicy Sausage
Rye Deckers: Herring and Beetroot, Liver and Lettuce

POTATO SAUSAGE LOAF

Makes approximately 16 slices
3 eggs, hard-boiled
1 × 440 g (15½ oz) can potato salad
200 g (7 oz) can pfifferlinge or whole mushrooms, drained and chopped
175 g (6 oz) bierwurst or extrawurst, diced
salt and pepper
40 cm (16 in) French loaf
50 g (2 oz) German butter, softened
6–8 lettuce leaves

Separate the yolks from the whites of the eggs, sieve the yolks into the potato salad and mix well. Chop the whites and add to the potato salad with the pfifferlinge or mushrooms, sausage and seasoning. Mix well together. Cut the French loaf along its length, leaving one side uncut. Scoop out the dough and butter the whole of the inside of the loaf. (The dough may be used to make fresh breadcrumbs and stored.) Line the cavity with five or six of the lettuce leaves and spoon in the potato–sausage mixture. Close up the loaf and wrap in foil. Place in the fridge to chill for at least an hour. Cut into slices to serve. Shred the remaining lettuce leaves and use to decorate.

Germany has one of the oldest food laws in existence. It relates to the purity of beer and was laid down in 1516. The Act still stands today and states that nothing whatever can be used in the brewing of German beer other than water, hops, barley and yeast. Real German beers made in the Federal Republic have a taste and flavour all of their own, and should not be confused with the German-style beers brewed in Britain under licence.

SALAMI AND CHEESE PASTRY LOAF

½ red pepper, seeded and finely chopped
½ green pepper, seeded and finely chopped
1 small onion, finely chopped
75 g (3 oz) German butter
100 g (4 oz) self-raising flour
175 g (6 oz) German tilsiter cheese, grated
50 g (2 oz) German salami, finely chopped
3 eggs, beaten
salt and black pepper
1.25 ml spoon (¼ teaspoon) paprika pepper

Very gently fry the peppers and onion in butter to soften them a little. Place the flour, cheese and salami in a bowl and add the vegetables and butter. Stir and add the beaten eggs and seasoning. Pour into a well-greased loaf tin and bake at 190°C/375°C/Gas Mark 5 for 50 minutes. Loosen the sides with a knife and leave to cool in the tin. Turn out and cut into slices to serve.

SURPRISE LAYER LOAF

1 small Victory loaf
50 g (2 oz) German butter, softened
1 large head chicory
1 box cress
100 g (4 oz) German tilsiter cheese, sliced
1 eating apple, cored and sliced
4 Bismarck herrings with onions, cut into pieces
½ small head celery, trimmed and chopped
mayonnaise to taste

Cut the loaf in half and scoop out the dough with your fingers. Use to make fresh breadcrumbs and store. Butter the inside of each half loaf. Fill each half in layers starting with half the chicory and cress followed by cheese and apple. Next, add the Bismarck herrings and celery and finish with the rest of the chicory and cress. Add a little mayonnaise with the salad layers as desired. Press the two halves of the loaf together and chill.

To slice and serve the loaf you will need a helper to hold a fish slice against the cut end. Cut through the loaf with a bread knife and lay each thick slice flat.

Pictured opposite, from left to right:
Surprise Layer Loaf
Potato Sausage Loaf
Salami and Cheese Pastry Loaf

PICNICS AND BARBECUES

PRESSED HAM AND TONGUE LOAF

225 g (8 oz) German cooked ham, thickly sliced and diced

225 g (8 oz) tongue, thickly sliced and diced

4 × 15 ml spoon (4 tablespoons) mayonnaise

2 × 15 ml spoon (2 tablespoons) gelatine, dissolved in
2 × 15 ml spoon (2 tablespoons) lemon juice

5 ml spoon (1 teaspoon) real German mustard

2 German pickled gherkins, chopped

15 ml spoon (1 tablespoon) capers, chopped

15 ml spoon (1 tablespoon) chopped fresh parsley

salt and pepper

50 g (2 oz) German tilsiter cheese

Mix all the ingredients together and spoon into a 450 g (1 lb) loaf tin. Press well down and place in the fridge to set.

SPICED EGG AND SAUSAGE PIE

Choose the sausage to suit your own taste but avoid those which contain a lot of garlic as they are not so good with the eggs.

400 g (14 oz) frozen puff pastry, thawed

2 large onions, finely chopped

15 ml spoon (1 tablespoon) cooking oil

350 g (12 oz) potatoes, diced

175 g (6 oz) extrawurst, finely diced

100 g (4 oz) German cervelat or salami, finely diced

5 ml spoon (1 teaspoon) hot paprika

salt and pepper

4 eggs

Roll out just over half the pastry and use to line a 20 cm (8 in) flan tin. Roll out the rest of the pastry and keep on one side to cover the pie. Fry the onions in cooking oil for 2–3 minutes. Add the potatoes and continue cooking for a further 2–3 minutes, stirring from time to time. Stir in the diced sausage, paprika and seasoning. Spoon the mixture into the lined flan tin. Spread out and make four hollows in the mixture. Break an egg into each hollow. Damp the edges of the pastry and place the second batch of pastry over the top and trim to shape. Fork the edges and prick one or two holes in the top. Bake for 30–35 minutes at 190°C/375°F/Gas Mark 5 until puffed up and golden. Serve hot or cold.

BLUE CHEESE AND SALAMI QUICHE

175 g (6 oz) shortcrust pastry

75 g (3 oz) Allgäu emmentaler, grated

25 g (1 oz) blue brie, chopped

150 ml (¼ pint) single cream

3 eggs, beaten

salt and pepper

25 g (1 oz) pilzkäse, grated or crumbled

50 g (2 oz) German salami or cervelat, sliced

Roll out the pastry and use to line a 20 cm (8 in) flan tin. Mix the Allgäu emmentaler and blue brie together and add to the single cream. Beat in the eggs and season. Pour the mixture into the flan case. Place on a tray and bake at 190°C/375°F/Gas Mark 5 for 30 minutes. Arrange the salami slices over the top of the flan and sprinkle with the remaining blue cheese. Return to the oven and bake for a further 20–30 mintues until set in the centre and browned on top. Leave to cool.

The Durkheim Sausage Fair is held on about 20 September each year. However, its name is a bit of a misnomer, for though you will certainly be able to sample plenty of sausages, wine is the real reason for the fair. It started life as a meeting for pilgrims to the shrine of St Michael in the town. Nowadays the fair is a popular folk festival.

SAUERKRAUT SALAD

100 g (4 oz) streaky bacon, diced

8 spring onions, chopped

3 × 15 ml spoon (3 tablespoons) cooking oil

450 g (1 lb) German sauerkraut

5 ml spoon (1 teaspoon) caraway seeds

pinch of salt, pepper and sugar

chopped fresh parsley, to garnish

Fry the bacon and onion in the oil for about 10 minutes until lightly browned. Sprinkle over the sauerkraut. Flavour with the caraway seeds and seasoning and garnish with chopped fresh parsley.

SAUSAGE AND PASTA SALAD

225 g (8 oz) pasta shapes or noodles, cooked

225 g (8 oz) bierschinken, cut into strips

1 × 210 g (7 oz) can pfifferlinge or mushrooms, sliced

100 g (4 oz) celeriac, cooked and cut into pieces

1 red pepper, seeded and cut into strips

lettuce leaves

Dressing

4 × 15 ml spoon (4 tablespoons) mayonnaise

2 × 5 ml spoon (2 teaspoons) creamed horseradish

5 ml spoon (1 teaspoon) real German mustard

Mix the pasta, sausage, pfifferlinge or mushrooms, celeriac, gherkins and red pepper in a large bowl. Mix all the dressing ingredients in another bowl and pour over the salad. Toss well and serve on a bed of lettuce.

Pictured below

TILSITER BURGERS

Hamburgers are always among the most popular items at a barbecue and the cheesy filling in these stuffed hamburgers comes as a nice surprise.

600 g (1¼ lb) minced lean steak

salt and pepper

25 g (1 oz) German tilsiter cheese, grated

4 German cocktail gherkins, finely chopped

5 ml spoon (1 teaspoon) Bavarian-style sweet mustard

Season the minced steak. Mix the cheese, chopped gherkins and mustard and shape into small balls. Take a quarter of the minced steak and shape it round one of the cheese balls, making sure that the filling is completely enclosed. Flatten slightly to give a good hamburger shape. Repeat with the rest of the mince to make four hamburgers. Grill over the barbecue for 3–4 minutes each side for medium-cooked hamburgers, longer if you like them well done.

Alternatively, make small round hamburgers and thread them on to skewers before grilling.

WESTPHALIAN POTATO PIE

225 g (8 oz) frozen shortcrust pastry, thawed

300 g (11 oz) potatoes, cooked and sliced

1 large ripe pear, peeled, cored and sliced

175 g (6 oz) Westphalian ham, thinly sliced and cut into strips

2 eggs, beaten

75 ml (3 fl oz) milk

1.25 ml spoon (¼ teaspoon) dried basil

salt and pepper

Roll out two-thirds of the pastry and use to line a 20 cm (8 in) loose-bottomed flan tin. Roll out the rest of the pastry to make a lid. Mix the potatoes, pear and ham and arrange in the flan. Beat the eggs with the milk, basil and seasoning and pour over the potato and ham mixture. Cover with the pastry lid, fork the edges and prick the top. Bake at 190°C/375°F/Gas Mark 5 for 35–40 minutes until golden in colour. Eat hot or cold.

Pictured opposite:
Westphalian Potato Pie
Sauerkraut Salad
Tilsiter Burgers

SAUSAGE KEBABS

350 g (12 oz) piece of schinkenwurst or bierwurst

100 g (4 oz) button mushrooms with the stalks trimmed

4 tomatoes, halved

15 ml spoon (1 tablespoon) cooking oil

5 ml spoon (1 teaspoon) dried mixed herbs

salt and pepper

Cut the sausage into chunks. Thread on to skewers with the mushrooms and tomatoes. Mix the oil and herbs and brush the kebabs all over. Sprinkle with seasoning. Place on the barbecue and grill for 5–6 minutes, turning two or three times during cooking. Serve with Beer and Mustard Sauce.

BEER AND MUSTARD SAUCE

Serve this tangy sauce with bratwurst or Sausage Kebabs. The sauce can be prepared in advance and heated through while the sausages are cooking.

1 onion, finely chopped

1 stick celery, finely chopped

15 ml spoon (1 tablespoon) cooking oil

150 ml (¼ pint) German beer

2 × 15 ml spoon (2 tablespoons) clear honey

15 ml spoon (1 tablespoon) real German mustard

juice of ½ lemon

salt and pepper

Gently fry the onion and celery in cooking oil for about 5 minutes until soft. Do not allow the vegetables to brown. Add all the remaining ingredients and season to taste. Bring the mixture to the boil. Simmer for 5 minutes and serve.

SAUERKRAUT BURGER RELISH

This makes an unusual topping for barbecued hamburgers.

100 g (4 oz) German wine sauerkraut
1 large German pickled gherkin, finely chopped
½ small red pepper, seeded and finely chopped
5 ml spoon (1 teaspoon) capers
1.25 ml spoon (¼ teaspoon) caraway seeds
25 g (1 oz) caster sugar
black pepper

Put all the ingredients together in a bowl and mix thoroughly. Transfer to a closed container and leave to stand in the fridge for at least 24 hours before using.

HAMBURGER STICKS

600 g (1¼ lb) minced lean beef
salt and pepper
4 × 5 ml spoon (4 teaspoons) coarsely ground black pepper
4 × 5 ml spoon (4 teaspoons) very finely chopped parsley
15 ml spoon (1 tablespoon) paprika pepper, mixed with a little ground chilli
15 ml spoon (1 tablespoon) curry powder

Mix the beef with the salt and pepper and shape into 16 balls. Coat four of them in each of the coatings and thread on to skewers, arranging four different-coloured balls on each skewer. Grill over the barbecue for 8–10 minutes, turning from time to time. Serve with Sauerkraut Burger Relish.

CANAPÉS AND FINGER BUFFET

STUFFED CELERY STICKS

German lumpfish roe looks like caviar, and though it does not have quite the flavour of its much more expensive counterpart, it is very good with quark and celery. It comes in both red and black varieties and a mixture of the two looks very dramatic.

1 head of celery
250 g (9 oz) German quark
1 × 50 g (2 oz) jar German red lumpfish roe
1 × 50 g (2 oz) jar German black lumpfish roe

Wash the celery and remove the leafy ends and any broken sticks. Cut each stick into three or four lengths and fill with a little quark. Top with one or other of the roes and arrange in an attractive pattern on a serving platter.

STUFFED ARTICHOKES

Teewurst would be my first choice for an unusual filling for artichokes, but if you cannot find any use smooth German liver sausage instead.

100 g (4 oz) German quark
100 g (4 oz) teewurst or smooth German liver sausage
15 ml spoon (1 tablespoon) chopped fresh parsley
15 ml spoon (1 tablespoon) chopped fresh chives
salt and black pepper
2 × 312 g (14 oz) cans artichoke bases, drained
6 stuffed olives, sliced

Mix the quark and teewurst or liver sausage with the fresh herbs and seasoning. Spread a little of the mixture over each artichoke base and decorate with a slice of stuffed olive.

STUFFED VEGETABLE PLATTER

Arrange the following three stuffed vegetables on a tray together. They will look most attactive for a party.

STUFFED MUSHROOMS

Makes about 36

450 g (1 lb) medium-sized button mushrooms
75 g (3 oz) Allgäu emmentaler, grated
25 g (1 oz) German salami, finely diced
1–2 × 15 ml spoon (1–2 tablespoons) mayonnaise
salt and black pepper
sprigs of parsley

Wipe the mushrooms clean and cut out the stalks. Mix the cheese and salami with sufficient mayonnaise to make a stiff paste. Season to taste and spread over the mushrooms. Decorate with sprigs of parsley.

SMOKED FISH GEMS

Makes 24

50 g (2 oz) German butter

50 g (2 oz) plain flour

250 ml (8 fl oz) milk

100 g (4 oz) smoked fish (mackerel, eel, cooked haddock or cod), flaked

75 g (3 oz) Allgäu emmentaler, grated

75 g (3 oz) German camembert or green pepper brie, finely chopped

1 egg yolk

salt and pepper

1 egg, beaten

50 g (2 oz) dry breadcrumbs

oil for deep frying

Melt the butter in a pan. Stir in the flour and then gradually add the milk. Bring to the boil, stirring all the time. Stir in the fish, cheese, egg yolk and seasoning. Leave to cool and place in the fridge overnight.

Flour your hands and shape the mixture into balls. Dip each ball first in beaten egg and then in breadcrumbs, making sure that it is fully coated. Quickly deep fry in hot oil. Do not leave in the hot oil for too long or the balls may split. Serve at once.

STUFFED HAM ROLLS

Makes about 40

4 large slices German cooked ham (approx. 175 g (6 oz))

225 g (8 oz) German quark

2 × 15 ml spoon (2 tablespoons) chopped fresh parsley

salt and pepper

1 bunch spring onions

Cut the slices of ham in half lengthways. Mix the quark, parsley and seasoning and spread a little of this mixture all over each half slice of ham. Lay two spring onions along the length of the half slices of ham and roll up. Cut into bite-sized lengths to serve.

STUFFED EXTRAWURST ROLLS

Makes about 40

225 g (8 oz) German tilsiter cheese, grated

2 × 15 ml spoon (2 tablespoons) German sweet and sour relish

5 ml spoon (1 teaspoon) real German mustard

4 large slices German extrawurst (approx. 175 g (6 oz))

2 large pickled gherkins, cut into long sticks

Mix the tilsiter, relish and mustard and spread a little of this mixture all over each slice of extrawurst. Lay sticks of gherkin on the slices of extrawurst and roll up. Cut into bite-sized lengths to serve.

STUFFED KASSLER ROLLS

Makes about 16

knob of German butter

15 ml spoon (1 tablespoon) milk

4 eggs, beaten

salt and pepper

5 ml spoon (1 teaspoon) dried tarragon

100 g (4 oz) kassler, thinly sliced

Heat the butter and milk in a pan and pour in the beaten eggs. Cook over a medium heat, stirring all the time, until the eggs are lightly scrambled. Remove from the heat and stir in the seasoning and tarragon. Leave to cool. Spread the mixture over each slice of kassler and roll up like a Swiss roll. Cut each roll in half and spear each half with a cocktail stick.

PUMPERNICKEL CANAPÉS

Pumpernickel bread makes an excellent base for cocktail canapés. Cut the slices into six squares or buy the ready-cut rounds. For a milder effect use vollkornbrot.

CAMEMBERT AND BRAZIL NUT CANAPÉS

Makes 20–24

175 g (6 oz) German camembert, rind removed

50 g (2 oz) Brazil nuts, roughly chopped

black pepper

5 slices pumpernickel or vollkornbrot

5–6 stuffed olives, sliced

Mash the cheese with a fork. Mix in the Brazil nuts and black pepper. Use this mixture to spread on the pumpernickel squares or rounds. Top each canapé with a slice of stuffed olive.

SMOKED EEL OR TROUT CANAPÉS

Makes 20–24

225 g (8 oz) smoked eel or trout, skinned and boned

12 stuffed olives, finely chopped

5 ml spoon (1 teaspoon) lemon juice

black pepper

25 g (1 oz) German butter, softened

5 slices pumpernickel or vollkornbrot

Mince the smoked fish and stuffed olives together and flavour with lemon juice and black pepper. Stir in the butter. Use this mixture to spread on pumpernickel squares or rounds.

TILSITER AND CURRIED PRAWN CANAPÉS

Makes 20–24

225 g (8 oz) peeled prawns

4–5 × 15 ml spoon (4–5 tablespoons) mayonnaise

2 × 5 ml spoon (2 teaspoons) curry powder

100 g (4 oz) German tilsiter cheese, thinly sliced

5 slices pumpernickel or vollkornbrot

Mix the prawns with the mayonnaise and curry powder. Cut the cheese to fit the pumpernickel squares or rounds and top with prawns.

Westphalia is the home of black bread and pumpernickel is probably the best known. It was a typical poor people's bread using a very coarsely ground flour so as to waste as little as possible. Once pumpernickel has been baked, the longer it is kept the better it tastes.

LANDBROT CANAPÉS

Fresh landbrot fried in butter makes an excellent base for canapés. Spread the butter on both sides of the bread and fry in a hot frying pan until golden in colour. Leave to drain and cool and cut into squares.

PFIFFERLINGE AND MUSTARD CANAPÉS

Makes about 30

1 × 210 g (7 oz) can pfifferlinge or mushrooms, finely chopped

2 × 15 ml spoon (2 tablespoons) German herb mustard *or* 15 ml spoon (1 tablespoon) German mustard and 15 ml spoon (1 tablespoon) German quark

black pepper

5 small slices German landbrot, fried in butter

1 canned pimento, chopped

Mix the pfifferlinge or mushrooms with the mustard or mustard and quark and season to taste. Spread the mixture over the slices of fried landbrot and cut each slice into six pieces. Arrange on a plate and decorate with pieces of chopped pimento.

AVOCADO CREAM CANAPÉS

Makes about 24

1 medium avocado

15 ml spoon (1 tablespoon) lemon juice or wine vinegar

50 g (2 oz) German quark

salt and pepper

4 small slices German landbrot, fried in butter

a little chopped parsley

Mash the avocado with the lemon juice or vinegar and rub through a sieve. Mix with the quark and seasoning and spread the mixture over the slices of fried landbrot. Cut each slice into six pieces and arrange on a plate. Decorate with chopped parsley.

SMOKED FISH CANAPÉS

Makes about 30

2 × 110 g (4 oz) cans German smoked sprats, sardines or mackerel, well drained

2 × 15 ml spoon (2 tablespoons) mango or mango and ginger chutney

black pepper

5 small slices German landbrot, fried in butter

15 small German gherkins, cut in half and then into fans

Empty the drained fish into a basin and mash well with a fork. Mix in the chutney and seasoning and spread the mixture over the slices of fried landbrot. Cut each slice into six pieces and arrange on a plate. Decorate with small gherkin fans.

61

STUFFED EGG PLATTER

Makes 16 stuffed egg halves

8 eggs, hard-boiled and halved
2.5 ml spoon (½ teaspoon) curry powder
4 × 5 ml spoon (4 teaspoons) German quark
4 sprigs of parsley
50 g (2 oz) Westphalian ham, sliced
2 × 5 ml spoon (2 teaspoons) real German mustard
black pepper
25 g (1 oz) German salami, very finely chopped
2 × 5 ml spoon (2 teaspoons) mayonnaise
salt
4 stuffed olives
25 g (1 oz) German dill gherkins (two cut in half and the rest finely chopped)

Mash the yolks of two of the eggs with the curry powder and 2 × 5 ml spoon (2 teaspoons) of quark. Spoon back into the four half egg whites and decorate with sprigs of parsley. Arrange on a large serving plate.

Chop the ham very finely, retaining two slices. Cut these two slices in half and roll up. Mix the chopped ham with two more egg yolks and mustard. Season with black pepper and pile back into the egg whites. Decorate with the rolled ham. Add to the platter.

Mash two more egg yolks with the salami and mayonnaise and season to taste. Spoon back into the whites and decorate with stuffed olives. Arrange on the serving plate with the other eggs.

Mix the chopped dill gherkins with the remaining egg yolks and quark and pile back into the last of the whites. Decorate with the halved gherkins and add to the platter.

FESTIVE BOWLE

Serves 8

This is the general name given to German punch bowls. They are usually made with a mixture of still and sparkling wines and are prettily decorated with fresh fruit in season. They are served to informal gatherings of friends with a selection of cocktail nibbles as shown opposite and, of course, pretzels. Alternatively, they may be served with a lavish cold meat platter.

1 small fresh pineapple *or* 3 fresh ripe peaches *or* 225 g (8 oz) fresh strawberries *or* a mixture of fruit, chopped
1 bottle Mosel wine, chilled
1 bottle Rhine wine, chilled
½ bottle sekt (German sparkling wine), chilled

Remove any stones from the fruit. Add the Mosel and Rhine wines and chill for at least 2 hours. Just before serving, add the sparkling wine.

ASSORTED SAUSAGE ROLLS

Makes about 40

400 g (14 oz) pack frozen puff pastry, thawed
3 German frankfurters
3 German bratwurst
175 g (6 oz) coarse German liver sausage
175 g (6 oz) extrawurst or bierwurst
real German mustard and relishes to taste

Roll out the pastry. Place the frankfurters and bratwurst on the pastry and cut out sufficient pastry to wrap them in. Dampen the pastry edges with water to seal. Cut each sausage roll into four pieces and place on a baking tray.

Cut the liver sausage and extrawurst or bierwurst into slices about 1½ cm (¾ in) thick and cut each one in half. Roll each semi-circle in pastry and seal the edges with water. Place on the baking tray with the others and bake at 190°C/375°F/Gas Mark 5 for 20–25 minutes until puffed up and golden.

For a change, spread the pastry with real German mustard or relish before folding it round the sausage and proceed as before.

MARINATED FRANKS WITH BACON

Makes 24

6 German frankfurters
150 ml (¼ pint) German apple juice
1 small onion, minced
15 ml spoon (1 tablespoon) tomato ketchup
5 ml spoon (1 teaspoon) real German mustard
1 clove garlic, crushed
juice of ½ lemon
2 × 15 ml spoon (2 tablespoons) vegetable oil
12 rashers streaky bacon

Score the sausages with a sharp knife and lay in a shallow dish. Put all the remaining ingredients except the bacon in a saucepan and bring to the boil. Simmer for 5 minutes. Leave to cool and pour over the frankfurters. Leave to stand in a cool place for at least 2 hours.

Remove the sausages from the marinade. Cut in half. Wrap a bacon rasher around each half and secure with a cocktail stick. Grill until the bacon is crisp and golden. Cut in half again and serve at once with German sweet and sour relish or mustard.

Pictured opposite:
Festive Bowle
Assorted Sausage Rolls
Stuffed Egg Platter
Marinated Franks with Bacon

FOOD FOR SPECIAL OCCASIONS

CHEESE SOUP

This is a lovely rich and creamy soup. It makes an excellent dinner party starter. For an easier everyday version see the recipe for German Brie and Onion Soup on page 29. If you do not like the slightly stringy effect of Allgäu emmentaler, use a creamier cheese such as pilzkäse or German blue brie. Remove the crusts and finely chop before adding to the stock.

1 × 290 g (10½ oz) can condensed consommé
175 ml (6 fl oz) water
100 g (4 oz) Allgäu emmentaler cheese, very finely grated
100 ml (4 fl oz) double cream
2 large egg yolks (size 1)

Place the consommé and water in a saucepan over a low heat. Gradually sprinkle in the cheese, stirring all the time. Bring the mixture to just below boiling point and remove from the heat. Beat the cream and egg yolks with a fork and stir into the soup with a wooden spoon. Return the pan to a low heat and continue cooking and stirring until the soup thickens sufficiently to coat the back of the spoon. Do not allow the mixture to boil or the soup will curdle. Serve in individual bowls with black bread.

STUFFED SALAMI FANS WITH PICKLE SALAD

You really need a fairly large diameter salami for this dish but 5 cm (2 in) salami can be used. In this instance simply fold the salami into a curved shell with the filling in the centre. Whatever the size of the salami, don't forget to remove the skin.

75 g (3 oz) frozen peas
75 g (3 oz) frozen sweetcorn
100 g (4 oz) German quark
2.5 ml spoon (½ teaspoon) mixed herbs
salt and pepper
16–20 thin slices (100 g (4 oz)) German salami, skinned
Salad
225 g (8 oz) German dill gherkins, thinly sliced
2 × 15 ml spoon (2 tablespoons) German sweet and sour relish
sprigs of watercress, to garnish

Cook the peas and sweetcorn in lightly salted boiling water until tender. Drain well and leave to cool. Mix with the quark, herbs and seasoning. Make a radial cut in towards the centre of each slice of salami and form into a cone. Fill with the vegetable and quark mixture and arrange on four small serving dishes. Mix the sliced gherkins and relish and arrange at the side of the salami fans. Garnish with sprigs of watercress.

BAVARIAN EGGS

Both Allgäu emmentaler and bergkäse can be used for this recipe. I usually serve it as a dinner party starter but it also makes a good light lunch or supper snack. In the latter case, use 6–8 eggs and double the amount of liver sausage.

4 eggs, hard-boiled
50 g (2 oz) German liver sausage
salt and pepper
25 g (1 oz) German butter
25 g (1 oz) plain flour
450 ml (¾ pint) milk
50 g (2 oz) Allgäu emmentaler or bergkäse, grated

Cut the eggs in half lengthways. Take out the yolks and place in a basin. Mash with a fork and mix in the liver sausage and seasoning. Spoon the mixture back into the egg whites and place the stuffed eggs in a shallow ovenproof dish.

Melt the butter in a pan and stir in the flour. Gradually add the milk, stirring all the time. Bring to the boil and cook for 2–3 minutes. The sauce should be fairly stiff. Stir in the cheese and season to taste. Pour the sauce over the stuffed eggs and bake at 200°C/400°F/Gas Mark 6 for 15–20 minutes until lightly browned. If necessary, flash under a hot grill just before serving.

WESTPHALIAN HAM WITH ASPARAGUS

This is a popular combination throughout Germany. Use fresh asparagus in season; otherwise, use frozen or canned asparagus.

350–450 g (12 oz–1 lb) fresh, frozen or canned asparagus
5 ml spoon (1 teaspoon) dried tarragon
4 × 15 ml spoon (4 tablespoons) mayonnaise
salt and pepper
225 g (8 oz) Westphalian ham, very thinly sliced

Cook the fresh or frozen asparagus by standing in a deep pan with a little boiling water in the base. Cover and simmer for about 10–15 minutes until the asparagus spears are tender. Drain, retaining a little of the cooking liquor, and leave the asparagus to cool.

Mix the dried tarragon with the retained cooking liquor and leave the mixture to cool. Drain well and mix the tarragon with the mayonnaise and seasoning.

Arrange the cooked asparagus and thinly sliced ham on plates with the mayonnaise in little pots at the side.

Westphalia is famous for its ham and black bread and the former is said to have been popular with the Romans. In Germany Westphalian ham is usually bought in one piece and sliced as required since most homes have a mechanical or, nowadays, an electric slicer.

BREMEN CHICKEN AND SHRIMP RAGOÛT

I first had this unusual combination of chicken, shrimp and sausage in a restaurant in Bremen and after some experimenting have been able to achieve a fair copy!

25 g (1 oz) German butter
15 ml spoon (1 tablespoon) cooking oil
225 g (8 oz) button mushrooms, sliced
4 tomatoes, skinned, seeded and chopped
150 ml (¼ pint) chicken stock
4 chicken breasts, boned and cut into chunks
3 × 15 ml spoon (3 tablespoons) soured cream
2 × 5 ml spoon (2 teaspoons) plain flour
salt and pepper
100 g (4 oz) peeled prawns
175 g (6 oz) jar German cocktail sausages

Melt the butter and oil in a large frying pan with a lid and gently fry the mushrooms and tomatoes for 3–4 minutes. Add the stock and stir well. Bring to the boil. Reduce the heat and arrange the pieces of chicken on top of the vegetables. Cover with the lid and cook gently for 45 minutes.

Mix the soured cream and flour to a smooth paste and add to the pan, stirring all the time. Bring to the boil and cook for 5 minutes or so until the sauce is creamy. Season to taste. Stir in the prawns and sausages and leave just long enough to heat through. Serve with new potatoes or rice.

PORK FILLET WITH PFIFFERLINGE

15 ml spoon (1 tablespoon) cooking oil
15 g (½ oz) German butter
600 g (1¼ lb) pork fillet cut into medallions
75 ml (3 fl oz) stock
15 ml spoon (1 tablespoon) lemon juice
210 g (7 oz) can pfifferlinge or sliced mushrooms
250 ml (8 fl oz) double cream
salt and pepper

Heat the oil and butter in a frying pan and fry the pork medallions for 4–5 minutes on each side depending on thickness. When they are cooked through, remove from the pan and keep warm. Drain off any excess fat and pour in the stock and lemon juice. Bring to the boil and add the pfifferlinge or mushrooms. Add the cream and seasoning and bring to the boil. Continue cooking until the sauce has reduced and is nice and creamy. Pour over the pork medallions and serve at once.

LAMB CHARLOTTE WITH PEACHES

The mixture of rye bread, mustard and parsley gives an unusual flavour to this popular British roast.

1 shoulder of lamb
salt and pepper
175 g (6 oz) German landbrot
1 onion, finely chopped
15 g (½ oz) German butter
4 × 15 ml spoon (4 tablespoons) chopped fresh parsley
15 ml spoon (1 tablespoon) real German mustard with herbs
1 × 450 g (1 lb) can peach halves, drained

Season the shoulder of lamb and place in a roasting tin. Roast at 200°C/400°F/Gas Mark 6 for 20 minutes per 450 g (1 lb) weight.

Rub the landbrot between your fingers or process in a blender or food processor to make breadcrumbs. Keep on one side. Gently fry the onion in butter until it is soft but not brown. Mix with the breadcrumbs and all the remaining ingredients except the peaches, and season to taste.

When the lamb has cooked for the required time, remove from the oven and spread with the bread and mustard paste. Place the peach halves around the outside of the joint, cut surface down. Turn the oven up to 240°C/450°F/Gas Mark 8 and roast for a further 10 minutes until the coating is brown and crisp.

The Germans are very fond of bitter–sweet mixtures such as pork with dried fruit, lamb with peaches and apples with potatoes or sauerkraut. Fruits such as apples and cherries are also used to make soups and though these are quite sweet they are still served at the start of the meal.

Pictured opposite:
Bremen Chicken and Shrimp Ragoût
Pork Fillet with Pfifferlinge
Lamb Charlotte with Peaches

VEAL ESCALOPES WITH CHEESE AND CERVELAT

600 g (1¼ lb) escalope of veal, beaten

salt and pepper

100 g (4 oz) German tilsiter cheese, thinly sliced

175 g (6 oz) cervelat, sliced

5 ml spoon (1 teaspoon) dried sage

25 g (1 oz) German butter

2 × 15 ml spoon (2 tablespoons) cooking oil

150 ml (¼ pint) German dry white wine

Season the escalope and cut into 12 pieces. Top each piece with slices of cheese and cervelat and roll up. Secure with half a cocktail stick. Sprinkle with sage. Melt the butter and oil in a pan and fry the rolls of stuffed escalope until browned all over. Add the wine and bring to the boil. Reduce the wine by one-third. Reduce the heat and simmer for 5 minutes. Remove the cocktail sticks from the rolls and serve with the pan juices poured over the top.

ROULADEN

4 slices topside of beef, thinly cut

2 × 5 ml spoon (2 teaspoons) real German mustard

salt and pepper

2 large onions, sliced

2 German pickled gherkins, cut into thin strips

50 g (2 oz) katenspeck or smoked streaky bacon, cut into thin strips

15 ml spoon (1 tablespoon) chopped fresh parsley

15 ml spoon (1 tablespoon) plain flour

15 ml spoon (1 tablespoon) cooking oil

1 carrot, sliced

150 ml (¼ pint) consommé or good beef stock

2 × 5 ml spoon (2 teaspoons) tomato purée

2 × 5 ml spoon (2 teaspoons) dried mixed herbs

4–5 × 5 ml spoon (4–5 teaspoons) cornflour

15 ml spoon (1 tablespoon) soured cream

Spread each slice of meat with a little mustard and season well. Mix a quarter of the sliced onion with the gherkins, katenspeck or streaky bacon and parsley. Divide the mixture into four portions and place one portion on each slice of beef. Roll up each slice and secure the ends with one or two cocktail sticks or tie up with cotton thread. Mix the flour with seasoning and dust each roll of beef with the mixture. Fry in hot cooking oil until brown all over. Add the remaining onions and the carrots and sauté for 2–3 minutes. Pour in the consommé or stock, tomato purée and herbs. Bring to the boil and simmer very gently for 1½–2 hours until the meat is tender.

Remove the beef rolls from the pan and take out the cocktail sticks or remove the cotton. Keep warm. Thicken the sauce with the cornflour. Bring to the boil, remove from the heat and stir in the soured cream. Correct the seasoning and pour over the beef. Serve at once.

CHEESY TARRAGON CHICKEN

The cheesy layer beneath the chicken skin both flavours the chicken and stops the flesh drying out.

1 roasting chicken (approx. 2 kg (4 lb))
4 × 15 ml spoon (4 tablespoons) German quark
4 × 5 ml spoon (4 teaspoons) chopped fresh tarragon *or* **2 × 5 ml spoon (2 teaspoons) dried tarragon**
salt and pepper
150 ml (¼ pint) German dry white wine
2 × 15 ml spoon (2 tablespoons) double cream
1 egg yolk

Wash and dry the chicken thoroughly. Ease the skin away from the flesh over the breast and top of the thighs, taking care not to split the skin.

Mix the quark, two-thirds of the tarragon and seasoning and spoon between the exposed flesh of the chicken and the skin, gently pulling the skin back into place.

Wrap the chicken in kitchen foil and bake at 190°C/375°F/Gas Mark 5 for 1 hour. Unwrap the chicken to expose the breast and return to the oven for a further 20–30 minutes to brown the skin. Drain off all the juices from the chicken and skim off the fat with kitchen paper. Pour into a saucepan with the wine and remaining tarragon. Bring to the boil and reduce by a third. Beat the cream and egg yolk. Remove the pan from the heat and whisk in the cream and egg mixture. Reheat gently, but do not allow the mixture to boil. Serve in a warmed sauceboat beside the bird.

DELICIOUS DESSERTS

APPLE DUMPLINGS

225 g (8 oz) plain flour
pinch of salt
100 g (4 oz) German butter
75 g (3 oz) sugar
2 eggs, separated
2 × 15 ml spoon (2 tablespoons) soured cream
4 small cooking or eating apples
4 × 5 ml spoon (4 teaspoons) jam
4 × 5 ml spoon (4 teaspoons) flaked almonds

Sift the flour and salt into a bowl. Cut the butter into small pieces and rub into the flour until the mixture resembles fine breadcrumbs. Stir in the sugar and then add the egg yolks and soured cream. Quickly knead to a smooth dough. Wrap in polythene and chill for 45 minutes.

Divide the dough into four and roll out each piece fairly quickly to make one round of pastry. Peel and core the apples and fill the centre of each one with jam and almonds. Wrap in pastry squares and cover the join at the top with a little round of pastry. Glaze with beaten egg white and bake at 180°C/350°F/Gas Mark 4 for 40 minutes.

BAKED RYE AND APPLE PUDDING

The use of wholemeal rye bread and sliced apples gives a new twist to the traditional bread and butter pudding. Use either vollkornbrot or, for a stronger flavour, pumpernickel.

4 slices (100 g (4 oz)) wholemeal rye bread such as vollkornbrot or pumpernickel
2 × 15 ml spoon (2 tablespoons) sugar
2.5 ml spoon (½ teaspoon) ground cinnamon
450 g (1 lb) cooking apples, peeled, cored and sliced
2 eggs, beaten
175 ml (6 fl oz) milk

Rub the rye bread between your fingers to make breadcrumbs or process in a blender or food processor. Mix with the sugar and cinnamon.

Sprinkle a layer of breadcrumbs over the base of a small pie or flan dish and cover with a layer of sliced apples. Continue these layers until all the ingredients have been used up. End with a layer of apple.

Mix the beaten egg and milk and pour over the top of the fruit. Bake at 190°C/350°F/Gas Mark 4 for 1–1¼ hours until the centre is set and the apples on the top are lightly browned.

APPLE AND RAISIN CURD TARTS

These little tarts are delicious served with fresh cream as a dessert or they can be served with afternoon tea.

225 g (8 oz) cooking apples, peeled, cored and sliced

50 g (2 oz) sugar

25 g (1 oz) raisins

225 g (8 oz) shortcrust pastry

25 g (1 oz) German butter

100 g (4 oz) German quark

3 × 15 ml spoon (3 tablespoons) soured cream

1 egg, separated

5 ml spoon (1 teaspoon) ground cinnamon

Rinse the apples and cook them on their own in a non-stick pan until tender. Beat with a fork to remove any lumps and mix in half the sugar and all the raisins. Leave to cool.

Roll out the pastry and use to line 12–14 deep bun tins.

Cream the butter and the remaining sugar. Add the quark, soured cream and egg yolk and beat to a smooth cream. Whisk the egg white until really stiff and fold into the curd mixture.

Place a small spoonful of the apple and raisin mixture in the base of each pastry-lined bun tin. Top with the curd mixture, making sure that the level is up to but not over the level of the pastry. Bake at 170°C/375°F/Gas Mark 3 for about 1–1½ hours, until well browned. When the tarts are cooked place on a wire rack to cool.

HANNAH'S APPLE DELIGHT

This crunchy dessert makes a good ending to a special meal. Serve it on its own or with whipped cream.

600 g (1¼ lb) cooking apples, peeled, cored and sliced

3 slices (75 g (3 oz)) wholemeal rye bread such as vollkornbrot

50 g (2 oz) German butter

50 g (2 oz) sugar

50 g (2 oz) plain chocolate, grated

2.5 ml spoon (½ teaspoon) grated orange peel

Place the apples in a saucepan with a little water and bring to the boil. Simmer for 5–6 minutes until the apples are cooked through. Sieve or purée in a blender and leave to cool.

Rub the rye bread between your fingers to make breadcrumbs or process in a blender or food processor. Melt the butter in a frying pan and fry the crumbs for 3–4 minutes until crisp. Leave to cool. Stir in the sugar, chocolate and orange peel.

Place a layer of the crumb mixture in the base of four individual glass dishes. Cover with a layer of apple and then another layer of crumbs. Repeat these two layers and serve.

If in doubt about where to eat in any large German city, try the Rathaus or town hall. Very often these will have an excellent restaurant in the cellar or basement where you can be sure of having a traditional German meal of very good quality. I can certainly vouch for those in Bremen and Munich!

BLACKCURRANT CHEESE MOUSSE

The use of low-calorie quark in place of cream in this recipe makes a deliciously light dessert which is excellent after a rich dinner. Top with fresh fruit when available or decorate with hundreds and thousands. Alternatively, make a flower pattern with sticks of angelica and crystallised violets.

200 ml (7 fl oz) blackcurrant nectar
½ × 15 g (½ oz) packet gelatine
50 g (2 oz) sugar
250 g (9 oz) carton low-calorie German quark
2 eggs, separated

Mix 3 × 15 ml spoon (3 tablespoons) of the nectar with the gelatine in a cup and place the cup in a pan of hot water. Stir until dissolved. Whisk the remaining nectar with the sugar, quark and egg yolks to form a smooth, frothy cream. Add the gelatine mixture. Whisk the egg whites until stiff. Stir 2 × 15 ml spoon (2 tablespoons) of the egg whites into the cream and fold in the rest. Pour the mixture into four individual glass dishes, a large glass bowl or a large fancy mould. Place in the fridge to set.

TRADITIONAL CHEESECAKE

This is just as good with a layer of fruit under the cheesecake. Use canned plums, strawberries or apricots.

Base
25 g (1 oz) German butter, melted
100 g (4 oz) sweet biscuit crumbs
Topping
100 g (4 oz) German butter
4 × 15 ml spoon (4 tablespoons) sugar
450 g (1 lb) German quark
300 ml (½ pint) soured cream
4 × 5 ml spoon (4 teaspoons) orange juice
2 × 5 ml spoon (2 teaspoons) grated orange rind
4 large eggs (size 1 or 2), separated

Mix the butter and biscuit crumbs and press into the base of a 23 cm (9 in) loose-based cake tin.

Cream the butter and sugar until light and fluffy, beat in the quark, cream, orange juice and rind and egg yolks. Whisk the egg whites until stiff and fold into the mixture. Pour into the cake tin and bake at 180°C/350°F/Gas Mark 4 for about 1¼ hours until set and golden brown on the top.

PEACH OR APRICOT TRIFLE

Trifle is almost unfailingly popular and this fruity version is no exception. For special occasions, add a little alcohol to the base: orange-based liqueurs go well with apricots, and kirsch is good with peaches. Use about a sherry glassful and pour over the sponge fingers with the fruit juice.

225 g (8 oz) dried peaches or apricots, soaked in cold water if necessary
150 ml (¼ pint) German peach or apricot nectar
12 sponge fingers or Boudoir biscuits
2 × 15 ml spoon (2 tablespoons) flaked almonds
1 × 425 g (15 oz) can custard
150 ml (¼ pint) double cream, lightly whipped
12–16 ratafia biscuits *or* 6–8 small macaroons

Drain the fruit if soaked and place in a pan with 50 ml (2 fl oz) of nectar. Bring to the boil, cover and simmer until almost all the liquid has been taken up and the fruit is tender. Leave to cool.

Arrange the sponge fingers in the base of a glass bowl and pour on the rest of the nectar (and liqueur if used). Arrange the cooked fruit over the top and sprinkle with almonds. Next add the custard and top with whipped cream. Decorate with ratafia biscuits.

SUMMER MOUNTAINS WITH SEASONAL FRUIT

150 ml (¼ pint) double cream
2 × 15 ml spoon (2 tablespoons) Black Forest kirsch or fruit brandy
15 ml spoon (1 tablespoon) sugar
100 g (4 oz) German quark
350–450 g (¾–1 lb) raspberries, strawberries, sliced peaches or kiwifruit
extra sugar, to taste
50 g (2 oz) flaked almonds, toasted

Lightly whip the cream with the liqueur and sugar and fold into the quark. Arrange layers of this mixture and fruit in individual glasses. Sprinkle with extra sugar, as desired, and toasted almonds.

Pictured opposite:
Summer Mountain with Seasonal Fruit
Blackcurrant Cheese Mousse
Apricot Trifle
Traditional Cheesecake

CRANBERRY AND PINEAPPLE FLAN

This is a lovely party dessert. It looks attractive and tastes delicious. This size of flan will serve 6–8 people. If you prefer to make your own sauce, use fresh or frozen cranberries with a little sugar syrup.

1 × 25 cm (10 in) sponge flan base
150 g (5 oz) jar or 5 × 15 ml spoon (5 tablespoons) cranberry sauce
350 g (12 oz) German quark
150 ml (¼ pint) double cream
1 × 400 g (14 oz) can crushed pineapple or pineapple chunks, well drained
8–10 walnut halves

Place the sponge base on a flat flan plate. Spread the cranberry sauce all over the base. This will sink into the base within about an hour to give an excellent flavour to the sponge. However, if you prefer a firmer base, make up the flan at the last minute. Mix the quark and 50 ml (2 fl oz) of the cream to a smooth consistency and spread all over the cranberry sauce. Next, add the crushed pineapple or pineapple chunks. Whip the remaining cream and pipe whirls around the edge of the flan. Decorate with walnuts.

74

PEACH SORBET

Peach nectar usually has the pulped fruit added to the juice and this makes it much thicker than nectars like the blackcurrant. Any of the nectars with added pulp would be suitable for this recipe. Shake the bottle or carton well before use.

| 150 ml (¼ pint) water |
| 50 g (2 oz) sugar |
| 250 ml (8 fl oz) German peach nectar |
| 1 egg white, stiffly whisked |

Place the water, sugar and nectar in a pan over a low heat and stir until the sugar has completely dissolved. Bring the mixture to the boil and simmer for 10 minutes. Leave to cool and then pour into a small rigid container and place in the freezer for about 2½ hours. The mixture should just be slushy and just starting to freeze. Fold in the stiffly whisked egg white and return to the freezer to set. Remove from the freezer and place in the fridge for about 20 minutes before using.

WAFFLES WITH BLACKCURRANT SYLLABUB

Syllabub makes a lovely light and airy accompaniment to hot waffles. It is also very good served in individual glass dishes with small wafer biscuits. My family like the flavour of blackcurrants but any fruit nectar could be used instead.

| 150 ml (¼ pint) German blackcurrant nectar |
| 2 × 15 ml spoon (2 tablespoons) Black Forest kirsch |
| 75 g (3 oz) sugar |
| 300 ml (½ pint) double cream |
| 4–8 frozen waffles |
| 4 × 5 ml spoon (4 teaspoons) blackcurrant jam |

Place the nectar, kirsch, sugar and double cream in a bowl and whisk until thick and frothy. Grill the waffles as directed on the pack and serve at once with the syllabub topping and a small spoonful of blackcurrant jam.

Coffee is certainly the national beverage in Germany and is drunk as the British might have a cup of tea — at every and any time of the day. The coffee is almost always 'real' coffee, prepared by the filter method.

DRINKS

BEER

No reference to food and drink from Germany would be complete without beer. If coffee is the West German's national beverage, then beer is the national drink. Three-quarters of all the breweries in the Common Market are located in the Federal Republic. And Bavaria in Southern Germany and its capital city, Munich, are often referred to as the brewing centre of the world.

Germany is justifiably very proud of its beer. Despite the fact that there are some 1500 breweries (1000 of which are in Bavaria!), the quality and 'taste' of German beers is universally first class. This is the result of Germany's oldest food and drink regulation dating from 1516, and still in force today, which stipulates that beer produced in Germany may contain only the natural ingredients malt, hops, yeast and water. No chemicals or other additives are permitted. The result is over 5000 varieties of beer, more than are produced in any other country in the world, and each one has its own subtle taste and flavour.

Despite the growing number of German-style beers brewed in Britain these days, exports of the real thing from Germany are increasing each year. Most German beer exported to the UK is of the lager type, though a far cry from the multitude of insipid lagers which flood many pubs and off-licences! Real German beers tend to be of medium to high alcoholic strength, and are of premium quality. And it is this quality which has made them so popular in this country.

For me, one of the attractions of German beer is that it goes so well with German food. It complements the lovely sausages and cheeses and can be served at a snack meal, as part of a more lavish cold buffet, or with hot dishes like the ones given earlier in the book.

Certainly beer and food are inseparable in Germany. Most German families tend to drink more beer than wine with a meal – wine is often drunk more as an aperitif or after meals. Indeed, in some parts of Germany the man of the family will drink a glass of beer with his second breakfast, usually eaten around 10 a.m. and consisting of bread, sausage and cheese – a habit not likely to be so popular in Britain!

But one habit from Germany which I do recommend is the eating of pretzels and German salted cocktail biscuits as nibbles while enjoying a glass of German-brewed beer. They are delicious.

SCHNAPPS

Schnapps is the collective and colloquial term for all colourless, grain spirits. There are three main types:

korn, which is neutral in taste;
steinhäger – often in attractive stoneware bottles – which is strongly flavoured with juniper berries and comes from the little town of Steinhagen in North Germany; and *kümmel*, which has the pronounced flavour of caraway seeds.

There's nothing so warming as a schnapps and beer chaser on a cold day. But it is important to drink the schnapps really ice-cold: put the bottle in the ice compartment of a fridge for at least half an hour before you want to serve it, and pour into tiny glasses.

FRUIT BRANDIES

Germany makes it own brandies, called weinbrand, and very good they are too. But fruit brandies are one of the things for which the Germans are world famous. They are all true distillates of the fruits themselves, not merely flavoured spirits. Mostly stone fruits are used; the fruit ferments and is then simply distilled – no additives such as sugar, water or colouring are permitted. Spirits made by this method are entitled to have the suffix 'wasser' (water) to their names. The best-known are kirschwasser (cherry) and Mirabellenwasser (Mirabelle plum).

With berries, a slightly different method is used to enable the fruit to infuse in alcohol and then be distilled. Fruit brandies made in this way can have the suffix 'geist' (spirit), such as himbeergeist (raspberry).

WINE

West Germany's ability to produce so many fine wines is quite amazing when you consider it is the most northerly of all the principal wine-producing countries in the world. But despite the apparently unfavourable geographical situation, other factors combine to give Germany unique advantages for growing vines, for instance soil rich in minerals, and a temperate and equable climate which allows the grape longer to mature than in other wine-producing countries.

German vineyards lie along the River Rhine and its tributaries. The Riesling is the great grape of Germany. It produces nearly all the best German wines. Other well-known grapes include the Sylvaner, Müller-Thurgau and Spätburgunder.

You could be forgiven for assuming that Germany produces only white wine. In fact the vast majority of wine in Germany is white, but there is a small proportion of red produced and even a tiny per centage of rosé. Sadly hardly any of Germany's red wines are exported. They tend to be of high quality and limited availability and the Germans, quite understandably, prefer to keep them for their own consumption. It's worth noting that the German Food Centre in Knightsbridge, London, which has the largest German wine and beer shop in Britain, always has a few German red wines in stock.

There are 11 wine-producing regions in Germany. The characteristics of the regions' wines vary enormously, and even wines from the same region can offer different and distinctive tastes and flavours. The following will give you a rough guide as to what to expect from those regions of Germany that export a reasonable quantity of wine, and whose wines you can therefore find in Britain.

Baden produces about 12 different varieties of wine, red and white. It is impossible to generalise about these wines: they vary from powerful, weighty and spicy wines that can be kept for many years to mild and elegant wines that should be drunk young.

Franconia white wines are known for their classic quality and are quite different from other German wines; they are generally quite dry, robust and fruity, and maintain a delicious flavour, and tend to be popular with regular wine drinkers in Britain. Franconian (Franken) wines, which come from vineyards in the valley of the River Main, are easy to recognise because they are all bottled in flagon-like, dark green bottles.

Mosel–Saar–Ruwer is a region of three rivers which produces some of the finest German wines of distinctive character. They tend to be fresh and delicate with a fine fruity flavour. Mosel wines are widely available in Britain, and generally come in long-necked, green bottles.

Rheingau wines are the product of some of the most favourable climatic conditions for growing grapes in Germany. There is good soil, lots of sunshine and protection from the wind. As a result the wines develop an exceptional body and bouquet, and are both fragrant and fruity without being heavy.

Rheinhessen is one of the largest wine-producing regions in Germany and its wines are the most exported of all German wines. Depending on how much you want to spend, you can choose from light, wholesome and pleasant table wines to full-bodied, heavier wines which would appeal to regular wine drinkers. Nierstein is one of the best-known (and easiest to pronounce!) wines from the Rheinhessen.

Rheinpfalz is a region which has a reputation for quality wines going back many centuries. Almost a third of all German wine is produced here, and there is considerable variation in style and quality. The lower- and medium-priced wines are excellent for drinking with a meal, whereas some of the more expensive wines really ought to be drunk on their own for full enjoyment.

Wines from all three Rhine regions come in brown bottles.

I'm not going to attempt to recommend which German wines go with which German food. It is so much a case of personal taste. The point about German wines is that there are many different types to choose from. So try lots of different ones and make a note of those you prefer.

As a rough guide to newcomers to German wines, those from Franconia tend to be consistently dry, followed by Baden and Mosel wines, through to the Rhine wines which are sweeter and have a lot of fruit.

And a special word for a very special wine, sekt, which is Germany's sparkling wine. Sekts, especially those exported, are of excellent quality and reasonably priced (particularly compared to champagne prices!). They have all the taste and flavour expected of German white wines, and make a delicate and refreshing drink, especially for parties and celebrations. If, as I do, you prefer dryer wine, look for those marked 'trocken', meaning dry.

There are wines from Germany to suit almost any pocket. Generally speaking, the higher the quality, the higher the price. The following is a list of the quality designations of German wines.

Table wines (*Landwein*) These simple wines are the most recent category of German wine to be officially designated. To qualify, all landwein must be made exclusively from grapes grown in one of 15 German landwein regions. They are all low in alcohol and range in taste from dry to semi-dry.

Table wines (*Deutscher Tafelwein*) Genuine German table wines must, by law, come from just four designated areas, Rhine/Mosel, Main, Neckar and Upper Rhine, and the appropriate identification must appear on the label. German table wines are light and perfect for everyday drinking. Try adding a little soda water for a refreshing and thirst-quenching drink.

Quality wines (*Qualitätswein*) Quality German wines are stronger than table varieties and reflect regional flavours. They are strictly controlled, even down to minimum alcohol content, and are often designated QbA on the label.

Quality wines with distinction (*Qualitätswein mit Prädikat*) Moving up the quality scale, there are a number of specially graded quality wines (also known as QmP) which are identified on the label by a number of grade descriptions. The most readily available in Britain, in order of quality, are as follows.

Kabinett wines, the basic QmP designation, are elegant, fully ripened wines, harvested at the 'normal' time, which is usually in October. This is later than in the rest of Europe. It is the lengthy, slow ripening time which adds to German wine's unique characteristics.

Spätlese wines are also wines from grapes picked at the 'normal' time, but they are identified for their special elegance and ripeness and are rich in character.

Auslese wines are produced from fully ripe grapes which are specially sorted from the rest and pressed separately. You can taste the ripeness of the grapes when you drink Auslese wines. The sweetness and the quality of the wine will be high.

Beerenauslese wines are for when you really want to indulge yourself! These wines are made from ripe and over-ripe grapes, separated by hand. The result is a wonderful, mature, fruity and full wine with an unmistakable flowery aroma and a colour like amber. Definitely wines for a special occasion.

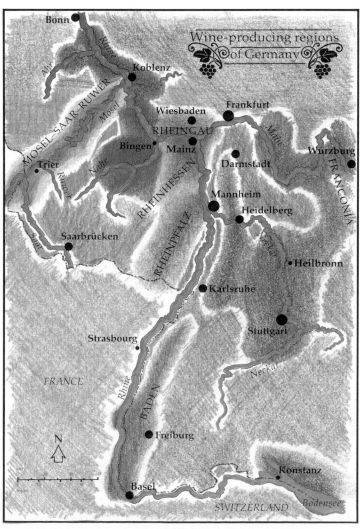

FEUERZANGEN BOWLE

Serves 8–10

This is a hot punch popular on cold winter evenings. Feuerzangen bowle is rather difficult to make in Britain as you need not only special equipment but also a special sugar cone made from pressed sugar and these have to be bought in Germany, or from the German Food Centre in Knightsbridge, London.

However, if you buy a feuerzangen bowle set on holiday the punch is made as follows.

3 bottles red wine
5 cloves
1 piece cinnamon stick
a little grated lemon rind
juice of 2 oranges
juice of ½ lemon
1 sugar cone
½ litre (1 pint) dark high-proof rum

Heat the red wine, spices and lemon rind in a pan. Stir in the fruit juice and pour into the copper pan of the feuerzangen bowle set. Place the sugar cone in the holder across the top of the pan. Spoon the rum over the sugar cone and set fire to it; the sugar will then melt and drip into the wine. If the flame shows signs of going out, add a little more rum. When all the sugar has melted, stir the wine and serve.

It is possible to use sugar lumps instead of the cone but it is not nearly so much fun. Simply add the sugar cubes to the hot wine with the rum and stir until fully dissolved.

GLÜHWEIN

Serves 6–8

This is another hot punch but it is much easier to make than feuerzangen bowle as you can purchase packets of special German mulled wine spices.

2 bottles red wine
3–4 × 15 ml spoon (3–4 tablespoons) sugar to taste
2 sachets German mulled wine spices

Place the wine in a saucepan with the sugar and heat gently, stirring until all the sugar has dissolved. Do not allow the mixture to boil. Pour over the sachets of mulled wine spices and leave to stand for 10–15 minutes before serving.

RUMTOPF

This makes a deliciously alcoholic dessert for festive occasions. You will not need to serve very much of it and a large jar should see you through the winter. In Germany they use beautifully decorated earthenware jars, but Kilner jars would be just as good. Start off with a wide-topped jar at the beginning of the soft fruit season and go on adding to the jar as the summer progresses. Make sure that the fruit is always kept below the level of the alcohol.

raspberries, strawberries, red- and blackcurrants, cherries and plums
175 g (6 oz) sugar to each 450 g (1 lb) fruit
dark rum

Wash the fruit and pick it over to remove any stalks or leaves. Remove the stones if present. Pack into the jar with layers of sugar and cover with rum. If the jar is not full to start with, use a small saucer with a weight on it to keep the fruit below the level of the liquid. Fill up with more fruit as the summer progresses. At the end of the season seal the jar to stop the alcohol evaporating.

Rumtopf is delicious served as a sauce with ice-cream.

There are many, many stories concerning the origin of pretzels. One story relates that a baker who lived at the foot of the Alps was thrown into prison on a charge of supplying bad bread. Only on one condition would he be freed – if he could succeed in baking something through which the sun would shine thrice. And so after lots of effort and many sleepless nights he came up with a pretzel!

Pictured opposite:
Feuerzangen Bowle
Glühwein
Rumtopf (served as a sauce with ice-cream)

COFFEE PHARISEE

There is a delightful story behind the name of this alcoholic coffee drink. It tells of a strictly teetotal preacher who took up a living in one of the islands off the northern coast of Germany. One day one of his parishioners decided to throw a party and invite the preacher. Everyone was served with coffee laced with rum except the preacher, who was served with coffee alone. As the party grew merrier the preacher received a glass of the laced coffee by mistake and was so angry that he insulted the host and called him a Pharisee and a hypocrite.

| 450 ml (¾ pint) strong black coffee |
| 4 × 5 ml spoon (4 teaspoons) brown sugar |
| 4 × 25 ml (1 fl oz) measures dark rum |
| 75 ml (3 fl oz) double cream, lightly whipped |

Pour the coffee into four heated glasses or cups and mix with the sugar and rum. Top with lightly whipped cream and a sprinkling of drinking chocolate and serve at once.

RUDESHEIM COFFEE

This is very similar to Coffee Pharisee, but unlike the rum drinkers of Northern Germany, the people of the Rhineland prefer brandy, no doubt because they make a fine, smooth brandy locally.

| 450 ml (¾ pint) strong black coffee |
| 4 × 5 ml spoon (4 teaspoons) brown sugar |
| 4 × 25 ml (1 fl oz) measures brandy |
| 75 ml (3 fl oz) double cream, lightly whipped |

Pour the coffee into four heated glasses or cups and mix with the sugar and brandy. Top with lightly whipped cream and serve at once.

BLACK FOREST COCKTAIL

The Black Forest is the home of fruit brandies. Think of a fruit and the Southern Germans will probably have thought of a brandy. They are all delicious served ice-cold on their own, but they also make first-class cocktails. Here's one I concocted at home with a pear brandy bought on a visit to Freiburg. Take care, it has quite a kick.

| slice of lemon |
| 15 ml spoon (1 tablespoon) caster sugar |
| 100 ml (4 fl oz) Black Forest pear brandy |
| 5 ml spoon (1 teaspoon) lemon juice |
| 25 ml (1 fl oz) dry vermouth |
| 6 ice cubes |

Prepare four glasses by rubbing the lemon round the rim of each one and dip in sugar to frost the edges. Place the remaining ingredients in a cocktail shaker and shake well. Pour into the glasses and serve.

SHADY LADY

This is a lighter, more fruity cocktail which makes use of one of the many fruit nectars made in Germany.

| 75 ml (3 fl oz) German apricot nectar, chilled |
| 50 ml (2 fl oz) schnapps, chilled |
| 1 bottle sekt (German sparkling wine), chilled |
| 4 ice cubes |

Mix the apricot nectar with schnapps and divide between four wine glasses. Top up with sekt and serve with an ice cube in each glass.

PEACH CREAM SODA

| 4 scoops vanilla ice cream |
| 450 ml (¾ pint) German peach nectar |
| 250 ml (8 fl oz) soda water or lemonade |
| 1 fresh or canned peach, finely chopped |

Place a scoop of ice cream in the base of each of four tall glasses. Divide the peach nectar between the glasses and top up with soda water or lemonade. Sprinkle the top with chopped peach and serve with a long spoon and a straw.

MILK SHAKES

Really fruity milk shakes can be made with the various German fruit juices and nectars on sale in Britain. Here's a basic recipe to try with your favourite juice. Add a little fresh fruit if you have it for a more interesting texture.

| 200 ml (⅓ pint) German fruit nectar (peach, apricot or grape) |
| 450 ml (¾ pint) cold milk |
| 1 scoop vanilla ice cream |
| a little fresh fruit, chopped |

Place all the ingredients in a blender or food processor and blend until smooth. Alternatively, mix with a hand whisk. Add only half the milk at this stage if using a food processor or hand whisk. Stir in the rest of the milk at the end.

Pictured opposite:
Shady Lady
Milk Shake
Peach Cream Soda
Rudesheim Coffee
Black Forest Cocktail
Coffee Pharisee

ENTERTAINING GERMAN-STYLE

Grüne Sauce was said to be a great favourite of Goethe's. The recipe did not originate, as is sometimes popularly supposed, from his mother's recipe book but from France. However, it has now become firmly established in the cooking of Frankfurt.

SPICED BRISKET OF BEEF WITH FRANKFURTER GRÜNE SAUCE

Serves 12 as part of a buffet

2 kg (4 lb) salted brisket of beef, boned and rolled

2 carrots, sliced

2 onions, sliced

2 bay leaves

8 peppercorns

6 cardamoms

3 cloves

Grüne Sauce

250 ml (8 fl oz) mayonnaise

50 ml (2 fl oz) German quark

2 German pickled gherkins, very finely chopped

3 × 15 ml spoon (3 tablespoons) chopped fresh parsley

3 × 15 ml spoon (3 tablespoons) chopped fresh chervil

2 × 15 ml spoon (2 tablespoons) chopped fresh basil

5 ml spoon (1 teaspoon) chopped fresh rosemary

salt and freshly ground black pepper

Place the meat in a large pan with the vegetables, herbs and spices. Cover with cold water and bring to the boil. Cover the pan, reduce the heat and simmer for 3½–4 hours. Remove the meat from the pan and place in a round dish just large enough to hold it. Place a flat plate on the top of the meat and place weights on this to press the meat down. Place in the fridge and leave for 24 hours. Carve thinly to serve.

To make the sauce, mix all the ingredients together 1 hour before serving. Chill in the fridge and serve with the meat.

PIQUANT PINEAPPLE SALAD

175 g (6 oz) extrawurst, cut into strips

6 German gherkins, cut into strips

1 small green pepper, seeded and cut into strips

1 small red pepper, seeded and cut into strips

15 ml spoon (1 tablespoon) capers

5 ml spoon (1 teaspoon) Worcestershire sauce

4 × 15 ml spoon (4 tablespoons) cooking oil

2 × 15 ml spoon (2 tablespoons) cider vinegar

pinch of caraway seeds

a few drops of Tabasco sauce

1 ripe pineapple

few sprigs of mint

Mix together all the ingredients except the pineapple and mint in a large bowl and leave to stand in a cool place for 2 hours.

Cut the pineapple in half lengthways and cut out the flesh. Keep the skins but discard the woody core and chop the remaining flesh and add to the salad. Spoon the salad into the scooped-out skins. Decorate with sprigs of mint and serve.

CHILLED BREAST OF CHICKEN AND HAM WITH ASPARAGUS SAUCE

4 chicken breasts

salt and pepper

1 × 340 g (12 oz) can green asparagus tips, drained

3 × 15 ml spoon (3 tablespoons) German quark

½ × 15 g (½ oz) packet gelatine

2 × 15 ml spoon (2 tablespoons) German dry white wine

4 slices German cooked ham

4 stuffed olives, sliced

8 small bay leaves

Season the chicken breasts and wrap in foil. Roast at 190°C/375°F/Gas Mark 5 for 45–50 minutes until completely cooked through. Leave to cool.

Sieve the asparagus tips or purée in a blender. Mix in the quark. Mix the gelatine with the white wine in a small cup and place the cup in a saucepan with a little hot water. Stir the gelatine until it dissolves and mix into the puréed asparagus. Skin the cold chicken and cut the slices of ham to fit on top of each piece of chicken. Cover neatly with the asparagus sauce. Use the sliced olives and bay leaves to make a flower motif on each breast and place in the fridge to set.

SAUSAGE BUFFET PLATTERS

Beautifully arranged platters of sliced sausages and cold meats are a feature of all German buffets. They are extremely versatile in that they can be served with a Festive Bowle or hot punch at an informal gathering of friends or they may grace the finest buffet. You can also tailor their contents to suit your pocket. Here are three examples, showing a fairly modest quartet, a more elaborate array and a really sumptuous selection.

SIMPLE SAUSAGE PLATTER

Serves 6–8 as part of a buffet

100 g (4 oz) German salami, sliced
100 g (4 oz) German cervelat, sliced
75 g (3 oz) German smoked cooked ham, sliced
75 g (3 oz) smoked beef or Westphalian ham, sliced
fresh parsley
1 tomato, sliced
2 pickled baby sweetcorn (maiskölbchen)
1 German pickled gherkin, cut into a fan

Fold the slices of salami and cervelat in half. Cut the hams or ham and beef to fit the size of your platter and roll up each piece. Arrange the meats on the platter and decorate with the parsley, slices of tomato, baby sweetcorn and gherkin fan.

PARTY PLATTER

Serves 8–10 as part of a buffet

100 g (4 oz) medium-sized extrawurst or bierwurst, sliced
175 g (6 oz) medium-sized schinkenwurst or bierschinken, sliced
175 g (6 oz) German salami, sliced
100 g (4 oz) lachsschinken, sliced
2 kiwifruit, peeled and sliced
1 tomato skin flower
2 stuffed olives, sliced

Roll up each slice of meat and arrange in concentric rings on a large round plate. Decorate the middle with slices of kiwifruit and the tomato skin flower, and scatter the slices of stuffed olive around the edge.

Most entertaining in Germany is very informal and the food is much more likely to be served in buffet style with everyone helping themselves than as a sit-down meal. Make up a cold sausage platter and add another cold meat dish and some salads and you will have a really attractive-looking spread to serve at even the most important celebration.

Start off by serving a German sparkling wine as a welcome drink and then move on to a Festive Bowle, a hot mulled wine or a selection of still white wines.

CELEBRATION SPECIAL

Serves 16–20 as part of a buffet

225 g (8 oz) German cooked ham, sliced
1 × 300 g (10 oz) can asparagus tips, drained
225 g (8 oz) Black Forest ham or Westphalian ham, sliced
175 g (6 oz) medium-sized German salami, sliced
100 g (4 oz) small extrawurst or bierwurst, sliced
100 g (4 oz) lachsschinken or kassler, sliced
225 g (8 oz) schinkenwurst, sliced
225 g (8 oz) sülzwurst (brawn sausage)
fresh parsley
1 egg, hard-boiled and sliced
2 tomato skin flowers

Cut the slices of German cooked ham in half and roll each one around an asparagus tip. Arrange these ham rolls at one end of an oval or rectangular platter. Fold the Black Forest or Westphalian ham into rolls and arrange half of these along the length of the platter from the ham and asparagus rolls. Make the salami slices into funnels by folding them twice. Arrange these on one side of the rolled ham and the extrawurst or bierwurst on the other. Next, add a row of rolled laschsschinken or kassler on one side and the remaining Black Forest or Westphalian ham rolls on the other. Fold or cut the schinkenwurst and sülzwurst in half and arrange in rows on the outside. Decorate with parsley, slices of egg and tomato skin flowers.

MELON AND CELERIAC SALAD

1 melon
1 small celeriac, sliced and boiled in water for 6 minutes
2 carrots, grated
juice of 1 lemon
1 green apple, cored and chopped
100 g (4 oz) extrawurst, skinned and cut into strips
2 or 3 shallots or spring onions, finely chopped
3 × 15 ml spoon (3 tablespoons) mayonnaise
2 × 15 ml spoon (2 tablespoons) German quark
salt and freshly ground black pepper
2.5 ml spoon (½ teaspoon) grated horseradish or dry mustard

Cut the melon in half. Scoop out the seeds and discard. Scoop out the flesh and dice. Cut the cooked celeriac into sticks and place in a bowl with the melon. Add the carrot, lemon juice and apple and mix well. Stir in the sausages and pile up in the melon halves. Mix all the remaining ingredients together and pour over the salad.

ROTE GRÜTZE

This is made with a mixture of summer berries and is a speciality of Schleswig-Holstein. It can be thickened with either semolina or cornflour, although the latter gives a smoother effect. In either case the dessert should not be set too hard. In the winter make this dessert with German bottled fruit.

450 g (1 lb) mixed blackcurrants, redcurrants, raspberries and cherries (halved and stoned)
300 ml (½ pint) boiling water
75 g (3 oz) sugar
25 g (1 oz) semolina or cornflour
2 × 15 ml spoon (2 tablespoons) red wine
2 × 15 ml spoon (2 tablespoons) German quark
4 × 15 ml spoon (4 tablespoons) double cream, lightly whipped
15 ml spoon (1 tablespoon) sugar
a few drops of vanilla essence

Add the fruit to the pan of boiling water and simmer until the fruit begins to soften. Mix the semolina or cornflour with the wine and stir into the mixture. Spoon into individual glass dishes and leave in a cool place. Just before serving, mix the quark, cream, sugar and vanilla essence and place a spoonful on the top of each dessert.

WINE CREAM

Serve this deliciously light dessert with a selection of pretty little German biscuits arranged in groups or patterns on the plate.

300 ml (½ pint) German white wine
1 × 15 g (½ oz) packet gelatine
3 eggs, separated
75 g (3 oz) caster sugar
2 × 15 ml spoon (2 tablespoons) lemon juice

Mix 3 × 15 ml spoon (3 tablespoons) of wine with the gelatine in a cup. Set the cup in a pan of hot water and stir until the gelatine has dissolved. Whisk the egg yolks with the remaining wine and gradually add half the sugar. Continue whisking until the mixture is thick and creamy. Whisk in the lemon juice and gelatine. Whisk the egg whites until stiff and then whisk in the remaining sugar. Fold the stiffly beaten egg whites into the lemon and wine cream. Pour into a glass serving bowl or into individual glass dishes. Place in the fridge to set. Garnish with julienne of lemon peel and serve with assorted German biscuits.

BLACK FOREST GÂTEAU

The principal ingredients for this delicious cake should be on sale in most stores stocking German food products. However, if you cannot buy the sponge layers (schicht-tortenboden), a 25 cm (10 in) homemade chocolate sponge, cut into three layers, will be just as good.

225 g (8 oz) plain chocolate
a jar of German sour cherries
3–4 × 15 ml spoon (3–4 tablespoons) Black Forest kirsch
750 ml (1¼ pints) whipping cream, whipped
1 × three-layer schicht-tortenboden or homemade chocolate cake

Using a potato peeler and with the chocolate at room temperature, shave the chocolate into thin curls and chill. Drain the syrup from the cherries and mix with the kirsch. Prick the cake layers with a fork and place one on a serving dish. Soak it with half the cherry juice, and then add a layer of cream and a third of the cherries, leaving 2.5 cm (1 in) margin. Repeat with the second layer. Position the third layer and press together. Cover the cake with 600 ml (1 pint) of the cream. Spoon the chocolate curls over the cake, and decorate with piped whirls of cream and the remaining cherries. Chill for 1–2 hours before serving.

Rote Grütze, a popular German dessert, originated in Northern Germany where it was eaten only by the servants. It was made from buckwheat and red fruit, topped with milk or cream. However, the colours of the dish appealed to the patriotism of the rich citizens of Hamburg whose local colours were red and white, and so the dish came to be served at the grandest tables.

Pictured opposite:
Rote Grütze
Black Forest Gâteau
Wine Cream

TRADITIONAL FESTIVE FOOD

CELEBRATION CANAPÉS

The most beautiful and elaborate canapés are on sale in specialist delicatessens in Germany. They are rather more substantial than the usual cocktail canapés but not quite so robust as open sandwiches. They are served on special anniversaries and feast days. They could form part of a cold buffet or they might be served in place of a starter at a celebration dinner. Here is a selection for you to make at home.

MOCK CAVIAR FINGERS

4 German pickled gherkins, finely chopped
1 bunch of spring onions *or* 1 small onion, finely chopped
350 g (12 oz) German quark
salt and freshly ground black pepper
1 × 225 g (8 oz) packet pumpernickel
1 × 50 g (2 oz) jar German black lumpfish roe
1 × 50 g (2 oz) jar German red lumpfish roe
½ lemon, very thinly sliced

Mix the gherkins, onion, quark and seasoning. Cut each slice of pumpernickel in half lengthways. Spread with the quark mixture and top half with black lumpfish roe and the other half with red lumpfish roe. Decorate with twists of very thinly sliced lemon.

SMOKED SALMON ROUNDS

225 g (8 oz) self-raising flour
2.5 ml spoon (½ teaspoon) salt
6 eggs
300 ml (½ pint) milk
knob of German butter
15 ml spoon (1 tablespoon) water
75 g (3 oz) smoked salmon, finely chopped
black pepper
sprigs of parsley

Sift the flour and salt into a bowl. Beat two of the eggs with the milk and gradually beat into the flour. Leave to stand for 1 hour. Very lightly grease a griddle or frying pan and use the batter to make 16 small, thick pancakes. Leave to cool. Beat the remaining eggs together and place in a pan with the butter and water. Cook until lightly scrambled. Leave to cool and mix with smoked salmon and season to taste. Pile the mixture up on the pancakes and decorate with sprigs of parsley.

Stollen, a fancy Christmas bread flavoured with candied peel, rosewater and spices, takes the place of the British Christmas cake. The first reference to the Christmas stollen was in 1329 and in those days it was symbolic of the Holy Child wrapped in a cloth. Until recently German housewives took great pride in their home-baked stollen, but today the ready-made cakes are so good that more and more people are buying them.

CUCUMBER CANAPÉS

½ large cucumber

100 g (4 oz) Westphalian ham, thinly sliced

1 × 85 g (3 oz) tube remoulade sauce or mayonnaise

Cut the cucumber into 5 mm (¼ in) thick slices at an angle to the length of the cucumber. Arrange the slices on a plate. Roll up half of each slice of ham into a cigar shape. Arrange one roll along the length of each cucumber slice. Pipe the edges with remoulade sauce or mayonnaise.

If you cannot get tubes of sauce or mayonnaise, buy it in jars or make your own and make a funnel out of a round of greaseproof paper, cut off the end and pipe through that.

COATED CAMEMBERT WEDGES

100 g (4 oz) German butter

100 g (4 oz) flaked almonds, crushed

15 ml spoon (1 tablespoon) brandy, rum or whisky

1.25 ml spoon (¼ teaspoon) ground coriander

5 ml spoon (1 teaspoon) paprika pepper

1 small German camembert (approx. 350 g (12 oz))

Mix the butter, almonds and brandy or other spirit together until fairly soft and creamy. Add the coriander and half the paprika and mix again. Cut the camembert into two rounds and remove all the rind. Divide the nut mixture into two and put a layer of the mixture on each half of camembert. Place in the fridge to chill for 1 hour.

Cut each half of cheese into eight wedges and serve surrounded with small cheese biscuits and pretzels.

SALAMI AND CHEESE VOL-AU-VENTS

1 packet frozen medium-sized vol-au-vents

Filling

50 g (2 oz) German butter

50 g (2 oz) plain flour

450 ml (¾ pint) milk

50 g (2 oz) German salami, finely diced

100 g (4 oz) button mushrooms, finely chopped

50 g (2 oz) sweetcorn

salt and freshly ground black pepper

2.5 ml spoon (½ teaspoon) real German mustard

pinch of dried mixed herbs

50 g (2 oz) Allgäu emmentaler cheese, grated

Cook the vol-au-vents as directed on the pack. To make the filling melt the butter in a pan and stir in the flour. Gradually add the milk, stirring all the time, and bring the mixture to the boil. Add all the remaining ingredients except the cheese and cook for 5 minutes, stirring from time to time. Stir in the cheese, correct the seasoning if necessary and spoon into the vol-au-vent cases. Serve at once.

Goose is the traditional Christmas dinner in Germany but it is also served at other times in the winter months. St Martin's Day on 10 November is one such occasion and many restaurants will feature it on that day.

SPECIAL OCCASION SOUP GARNISHES

In many homes in Germany the Christmas dinner will commence with a rich, clear soup such as a beef consommé or a chicken broth. But to make it just a little more festive it will be garnished with small sliced pancakes, egg stars or tiny liver dumplings. Here are some ideas to try. The soups taste even better with a splash of sherry in them.

CARAWAY PANCAKES

100 g (4 oz) plain flour

salt

2 eggs, beaten

250 ml (8 fl oz) milk

1.5 ml spoon (¼ teaspoon) caraway seeds

Sift the flour and salt into a bowl. Add the eggs and a little of the milk and beat to a smooth consistency. Stir in the rest of the milk and the caraway seeds and leave to stand for 1 hour. Stir and place spoonfuls on a lightly oiled and heated frying pan. Make 6–8 pancakes and leave to cool. Cut into strips and drop into the clear soup just before serving.

LIVER DUMPLINGS

225 g (8 oz) lamb's liver, minced

1 clove garlic, peeled and crushed

25 g (1 oz) German butter, softened

salt and pepper

1 egg

175 g (6 oz) breadcrumbs

flour

Mix the liver and garlic. Beat the butter and seasoning with the egg. When well beaten, add the liver and breadcrumbs. Mix everything to a thick paste. With floured hands, shape the mixture into small balls and poach in boiling, salted water for 5 minutes. Drain and serve in clear soup.

EGG STARS

2 egg yolks

salt and pepper

2 × 15 ml spoon (2 tablespoons) milk

Beat the egg yolks with the seasoning and milk and pour into a greased bowl. Cover with buttered paper or foil. Stand the basin in a pan of simmering water and leave for 8–10 minutes until firm. Leave to cool and then turn out. Cut the custard into thin slices and cut into star or fancy shapes with petits fours cutters. Add to clear soups.

SEAFOOD PLATTER

This is another popular type of appetiser to serve at the start of a special meal or at a Christmas or New Year buffet.

1 × 113 g (4 oz) can mussels in tomato sauce

1 × 113 g (4 oz) can mackerel appetiser

1 × 133 g (4 oz) can cod liver, drained

175 g (6 oz) Bismarck herrings, drained and chopped

175 g (6 oz) smoked mackerel, trout or eel, cut into pieces

100 g (4 oz) German matjes herrings, drained and chopped

4 × 5 ml spoon (4 teaspoons) creamed horseradish

4 × 5 ml spoon (4 teaspoons) cranberry sauce

15 ml spoon (1 tablespoon) mayonnaise

2.5 ml spoon (½ teaspoon) curry powder

½ lemon, sliced

sprigs of dill or parsley

Arrange all the fish in an attractive pattern on a large flat serving dish and decorate with mounds of horseradish and cranberry sauce. Mix the mayonnaise and curry powder and put spoonfuls on the cod liver. Garnish the platter with slices of lemon and sprigs of dill or parsley. Serve with rye bread.

FESTIVE FISH

A special herring salad at Christmas time is a 'must' for most German families. It will be made in advance and in large quantities and may be served as a quick luncheon or supper dish, as the starter to a larger meal or just as a good snack to counteract the excesses of other Christmas meals. Every family will have its own recipe. This one is my favourite.

225 g (8 oz) Bismarck herrings plus their onions, cut into pieces

1 large green apple, cored and diced

4 German pickled gherkins, diced

15 ml spoon (1 tablespoon) capers

2 × 15 ml spoon (2 tablespoons) small silver cocktail onions

300 ml (½ pint) soured cream

2 × 15 ml spoon (2 tablespoons) mayonnaise

freshly ground black pepper

Place all the ingredients in a bowl and toss well together. Chill and serve on a bed of green salad with toast or with crusty rolls.

ROAST GOOSE

Serves 8

Goose is making a bit of a comeback in Britain and is quite easy to find around Christmas time, so why not follow the Germans' lead and serve roast goose with chestnut stuffing, glazed apples and red cabbage?

1 × 4.5 kg (10 lb) goose with giblets
plain flour
salt and pepper
Chestnut Stuffing
450 g (1 lb) chestnuts
milk
50 g (2 oz) katenspeck or streaky bacon, diced
1 large onion, finely chopped
25 g (1 oz) German butter
2 eggs
75 g (3 oz) fresh breadcrumbs
salt and pepper
2 × 15 ml spoon (2 tablespoons) chopped fresh parsley
5 ml spoon (1 teaspoon) dried mixed herbs
salt and freshly ground black pepper

Remove the neck, giblets and all the fat from the body cavity of the goose. Wash well and dry. Place the giblets in a pan with a little water, bring to the boil and simmer until tender.

Peel the chestnuts and place in a pan. Just cover with milk and bring to the boil. Simmer until tender. Chop the cooked giblets, retaining the cooking liquor, and mash the chestnuts with the milk they were cooked in. Mix well together.

Fry the katenspeck or bacon and onion in butter until soft and mix with the chestnuts and giblets. Add all the remaining ingredients and use to stuff the goose. Alternatively, press into an earthenware dish and bake separately.

Rub the goose all over with a little flour and season well. Prick the skin all over with a fork. Place on a rack, breast side down, in a roasting tin and roast at 220°C/425°F/Gas Mark 7 for 20 minutes. Reduce the heat to 180°C/350°F/Gas Mark 4 and continue cooking for 1½ hours, removing the fat from the roasting tin from time to time. Turn the bird the right way up and continue cooking for a further hour or so until the goose is cooked through. Test the leg with a fork: if the juices run clear, the goose is cooked. If the breast starts to show signs of drying up, cover with a little foil. Skim all the fat from the juices and pour in the giblet stock. Boil rapidly to reduce by about a quarter. Serve in a gravy boat with the goose.

GLAZED APPLES

4 cooking apples, peeled and quartered
4 cloves
150 g (5 oz) brown sugar
150 ml (¼ pint) warm water
juice of 1 lemon
3 × 15 ml spoon (3 tablespoons) dark rum
grated lemon rind
1.25 ml spoon (¼ teaspoon) cinnamon

Place the apples in a shallow baking dish and add the cloves. Dissolve 75 g (3 oz) sugar in the warm water and pour over the apples with the lemon juice. Bake at 180°C/350°F/Gas Mark 4 with the goose for about 30 minutes until soft. Sprinkle all the remaining ingredients with the remaining sugar over the top and place under a hot grill until the sugar starts to caramelise. Serve at once.

SPICED RED CABBAGE

The spices used to flavour this very popular dish vary in different parts of Germany. Here are two versions for you to try. Serve with all kinds of sausage, braised pork knuckle and duck or goose. If you are in a hurry, try making these recipes with one of the excellent German cans of cooked red cabbage. Continue as directed but cook the mixture for only 30 minutes.

15 ml spoon (1 tablespoon) cooking oil *or* 15 g (½ oz) lard
1 large onion, sliced
450 g (1 lb) red cabbage, shredded
2 × 15 ml spoon (2 tablespoons) vinegar
150 ml (¼ pint) water or German dry white wine
3 cooking apples, peeled, cored and sliced
Spices 1
3–4 cloves
1 bay leaf
pinch of sugar
salt
or Spices 2
5 ml spoon (1 teaspoon) ground coriander
2.5 ml spoon (½ teaspoon) cinnamon
1.25 ml spoon (¼ teaspoon) mace *or* pinch of nutmeg
2.5 ml spoon (½ teaspoon) grated orange rind
salt

Heat the oil or lard in a large pan and fry the onion until golden in colour. Add the cabbage and continue cooking for 3–4 minutes. Pour in the vinegar and water or wine and add the apples and your chosen spices. Bring to the boil, cover and simmer very gently for at least 1½ hours. Stir from time to time and check that the cabbage is not boiling dry. Add a little more liquid if necessary.

Pictured opposite:
Spiced Red Cabbage
Roast Goose
Glazed Apples

GINGERBREAD HOUSE

Gingerbread
1 kg (2 lb) honey
250 ml (8 fl oz) water
650 g (1 lb 7 oz) rye flour
600 g (1 lb 5 oz) wheat flour
35 g (1½ oz) ground ginger
15 ml spoon (1 tablespoon) mixed spice
25 g (1 oz) baking powder
18 blanched almonds (approx. 15 g (½ oz))
Icing
2 × 15 ml spoon (2 tablespoons) lemon juice
3 egg whites
350 g (12 oz) icing sugar
Decoration
sweets
German biscuits
icing sugar

Put the honey and water in a saucepan and bring to the boil, stirring all the time, until the honey has dissolved. Set aside to cool.

Sift the flours, ginger, mixed spice and baking powder into a large bowl. Make a well in the middle and gradually add the cooled honey. Knead to a smooth dough. Cover the dough and leave it to stand for 24–48 hours.

Following the diagrams opposite, make paper patterns of the pieces of gingerbread needed to make the house. Grease two baking sheets. Heat the oven to 200°C/400°F/Gas Mark 6.

Take just less than half the dough and form it into long thin rolls about 1 cm (½ in) in diameter and 46 cm (18 in) long. Use these rolls to form a rectangle measuring approximately 46 × 39 cm (18 × 15½ in), leaving 3 mm (⅛ in) between the rolls. (The gaps will close up during baking.) Bake for 20–25 minutes. Remove from the oven and, using the paper patterns, cut out the pieces for the front, back and side walls of the house. Cut out a door and window in the front wall.

Roll out the rest of the dough to a thickness of about 5 mm (¼ in) and cut out the pieces for the roof and base. Prick all over with a fork and bake for 12–15 minutes.

Roll the remaining dough to a thickness of about 5 mm (¼ in). Cut out 18 small gingerbread rectangles approximately 4 × 2 cm (1½ × ¾ in) and press an almond on to each one. Also cut out a chimney and thin strips for the fence. Bake for 12–15 minutes.

To make the icing, stir together the lemon juice, egg whites and sifted icing sugar. Using the photograph as a guide, stick the pieces of the house together with the icing and construct the fence. Decorate the house with sweets and German biscuits, such as lebkuchen hearts, spekulatius, printen and dominosteine, sticking them on with drops of icing. (Packets of these German biscuits are readily available in shops here at Christmas.) Any remaining icing can be piped on to the door and windows and used for snow on the roof. Sift a little extra icing sugar over the roof.

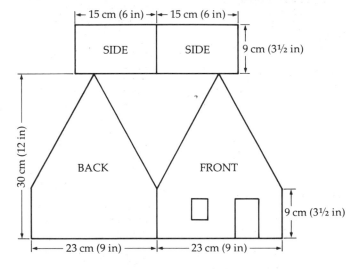

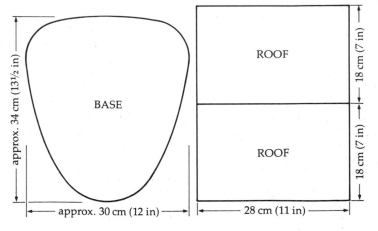

94

INDEX